# Teachers and Learners

Second Edition

# Teachers and Learners
## The Interactive Process of Education

ALFRED H. GORMAN

*Montclair State College*
*New Jersey*

Allyn and Bacon, Inc.   Boston

# Contents

# Figures

# Preface

This is a book for teachers who wish to improve that area of teaching that lies within the sphere of interactive behavior in the classroom. The basic assumption underlying the material to follow is that teaching and learning is a process of communication among individuals in a group setting. If such an assumption is a valid one, it follows as a first step that a professional teacher should be aware of theory and practice in human communication. As a second step he must then seek to internalize the material into his behavioral repertoire.

To accomplish such internalization—whether the book is used in a college classroom, in an in-service education program, or by an individual teacher—it is suggested that the material be treated in four successive stages. First, the book should be read carefully and discussed. Second, the class (including its teacher) should try out some of the exercises including reactions to them. Third, the materials should be reviewed to check as to whether understanding of them has been deepened by the exercises. Fourth, class members should attempt, perhaps after further reading in the field, to produce approaches and exercises adapted to their own personal needs. Where it is possible, a fifth step would include trying out some of these approaches in a practice-teaching situation.

Thus the teacher—or prospective teacher—dealing personally with interactive experiences should begin to develop skills both for communicating his knowledge of subject matter and for setting the classroom stage for student learning. In turn, this stage setting should create a readiness for teaching and learning by reducing the social distance between teacher and student while maintaining mutual respect.

Such a notion is certainly not a new or even an unusual one. Great teachers have always been able to cut through barriers to communication and reach their students. In addition, they have been personally flexible enough to allow their students to reach them.

One central value in all good teaching is that of student growth toward greater maturity and self-direction. This growth can be enhanced or inhibited to a marked degree by teacher behavior in and out of the classroom. When inhibition results, the teacher has not touched the student and the student has not really touched—or been touched by—the subject matter.

Teachers throughout recorded history have tried in various ways to reach their students, yet problems of passive learners and dominating teachers still exist. In the American society, which attempts education for *all* its youth, these problems have become more and more acute. The culturally deprived child, the growth of a delinquent subculture, the increasing numbers of dropouts, the racial minorities who seek integration into the larger society, the underachieving college-bound—all these youngsters present the school with an acute challenge that cannot be ignored or relegated to theorizing. It is for the teacher who recognizes these problems and who seeks specific answers to the question, "What can I do to reach my students?" that this book has been written. Its objective is the clarification in behavioral terms of just what does happen when students and teachers interact and how this happening can be examined, evaluated, and improved.

Materials are organized under three main headings: (1) the past, present, and future of teaching and learning behavior; (2) a conceptual framework for the teaching act; and (3) methods of approaching, developing, elaborating, evaluating, and improving classroom communication on both intellectual and emotional levels. Since the subject under discussion is interactive behavior, such important aspects of teacher education as philosophy, psychology of the learner, daily and unit lesson planning, curriculum construction, textbook selection, test construction, reporting of pupil progress, and the like are *not* dealt with here. It is assumed that they will receive their proper amount of attention elsewhere.

All the approaches detailed in the following chapters have been tested by the author in group learning situations. While they by no means constitute a bag of tricks that will work for anyone in any situation, they have proved useful in opening many new avenues of communication for teachers and students.

Effective teaching is always a difficult and demanding enterprise. If it were an easy one, there would be far fewer poor teachers and frustrated students. More often than not, however, "poor teaching" is really the existence of an interaction problem that is allowed to go unresolved. The material in this book does not do away with problems, but it does suggest ways in which they can be faced, defined, and solved. The reader who wishes to master this material can expect hard work, an intellectual and emotional challenge, and some frustrations and failures along the way. But if he is able to internalize and use the theory and methodology, he can also expect the greatest reward of teaching —the feeling that he has helped others to personal growth.

Alfred H. Gorman

# Teachers and Learners

# chapter 1

# Teaching and Learning:
## *Past, Present, and Future*

One of the most interesting characteristics of human life on earth has been its aggregate[1] composition. Males and females have had to be together to begin new life and have produced, generally, one highly vulnerable, dependent offspring at a time in two-year periods during the first twenty years of union. From the need to protect the young and to survive in an often hostile physical environment, the family aggregation formed as a natural response. The mother's role became that of child rearer and homemaker; the father's role became that of protector and food gatherer; and each child's role became, as rapidly as possible, a duplicate of the parent of the same sex. To help youngsters assume these adult roles, fathers and mothers—and older siblings—also had to become teachers.

Family aggregates saw early the advantages of combining with others and, as populations grew, formed bands, tribes, kingdoms, and nations. Such larger formations, and the developing technologies necessary to support them, allowed men to move from caves to skyscrapers, from club weapons to nuclear

---

[1] The reader will note that the term *aggregate* has been used in place of the more familiar *group*. This is a special use of the term by the author and is developed further on pp. 3-8.

bombs, from forest trails to superhighways, and from the self-sufficient aggregate to the age of the adult specialist with accompanying phenomenon of longer and longer years of enforced, dependent childhood.

Developing societies—faced with the problem of transmitting growing amounts of knowledge, skills, and understandings to their young—built schools and provided trained specialists to staff them. The family shared increasing amounts of its teaching responsibilities with outsiders and became even more of an aggregate than it had been. When employment patterns began to force father—and sometimes mother—to leave the home for work, the opportunities for the family to become more a group than an aggregate were further decreased.

As generation after generation added to knowledge of the physical world and to technologies to put this knowledge to work, the task of inducting the young of a society into its culture became more time-consuming. Schools, which began as agencies for a small percentage of children for a few years of their lives, were forced to expand and deal with more and more children for more and more years. In twentieth century America, the dream of schooling for all has become an increasing reality with each passing decade and additional years are still being added. The present standard of twelve years of public schooling is being increased at one end by kindergarten and nursery programs and at the other by junior or community colleges where transfer to a senior college is a growing option.

Almost overwhelming numbers of clients have filled the schools, and educators have been hard pressed to meet their needs and expectations. Combine the logistics problem with a knowledge explosion and a culture in a constant state of change, mix in an administrative and teaching group who, at least historically, have tended to resist change, and many highly frustrating problems emerge.

In attempting to deal with these problems, educators have struggled with their college-preparing, past-oriented institutions to bring them further into the present and point them toward the future. This is a task of staggering proportions, the solution of which will depend on defining current cultural values in operational terms. What kind of society do we want? What knowledge and what skills are of most value? What is the role of the school both in hammering out answers to the questions and in producing educational content and teaching methodology which is relevant, meaningful, and motivational?

This is a big job, and it is easy to avoid facing it. But the pressures now building in the society leave educators little choice. Help should come from the general public, parents of present students, and school board members. It should come from business and professional sources at the national, state, and local levels. It should come from educational theorists and from those who direct programs of teacher education. It should progress interactively throughout the professional staffs of local school systems to affect directly the climate and activities of the classroom teacher and his students.

At the cutting edge of action and of change stands the classroom teacher. It is this teacher to whom this book is primarily addressed. Since teachers—and students—depend to a great extent on the knowledgeable and skillful support of the entire staff, it is also addressed to those in areas of administration, supervision, health, guidance, and special support services such as custodians, crossing guards, lunchroom supervisors, secretaries, and others who make up the adult component of the school culture.

## Aggregates and Groups

The name of the game—as it always has been—is communication. *All* those involved directly in the educational process need to communicate face-to-face and decide jointly what schooling is to be like and how it will be accomplished. This, of course, will mean some lowering of traditionally rigid status barriers and the granting to all—including teachers and students—of first-class citizenship within the school. Such a movement is in line with newer cultural imperatives involving Afro-Americans, American Indians, women as a minority group, and the urban and rural poor. For the school to present itself as a democratic institution and a mirror of its society while holding fast to inherently autocratic processes in its own operation is both stupid and self-defeating.

Reference to autocratic behavior in the schools is not an attempt on the author's part to make scapegoats of educationists. They have faced and are facing a most difficult, frustrating task, and many of their responses have been excellent. Administrators are increasingly learning, and using, modern management techniques which involve greater numbers of staff in problem solving and decision making. Lockstep education has been challenged by daring alternatives such as the Parkway Project in Philadelphia, and in various parts of the country students are being invited to participate in curriculum studies and to sit with boards of education. The point is not that educationists are undemocratic but that democracy depends upon hard work, constant reexamination of ends and means, and the development of modern means based on current findings. It is with one of these means—*affect education*—that this book is concerned.

Affect education has its focus on human emotions and on ways in which people can interact emotionally with increasing effectiveness, expressing their own feelings and reacting helpfully to the expressed feelings of others. The historical concentration on *cognitive education* (dealing with facts, ideas, and concepts) has left people to learn *affectively* in a hit-or-miss, trial and error way. This unbalanced stress on the cognitive aspects of education has helped man create great technological societies, but it has offered little or no aid to self-understanding or to getting along with others. Modern education cannot afford to neglect *cognitive* education, but it is becoming clear that it must also address itself to *affective* education and achieve a balance between the two. Anyone (a teacher) communicating with anyone else (a student) needs to be constantly in touch with both cognitive (thinking) and affective (feeling) components. The notion of insisting that the teacher and students leave their feelings outside when they enter a room to teach or to learn is manifestly absurd. All it accomplishes is to force feelings underground from where they may surface as behavior problems and/or learning difficulties.

Any classroom scene—whether elementary, secondary, or college level—includes an aggregation of students with one or more special members called teachers. Use of *aggregate* for family and classroom in this chapter is a deliberate attempt to focus on the notion of *group*, and the difference between these two terms will be developed further in later chapters. At this point, it might be well to begin some definition since the notion of *group* is a central one in the book.

## Definition of Terms

A collection of people together in time and space is called an *aggregate* to indicate that they have not worked through "ice-breaking" introductory ceremonies, developed mutually agreed upon norms of behavior, and reduced those barriers to communication which are based on fear, suspicion, uncertainty, and lack of mutual trust. In the first paragraphs of this chapter, the family is referred to as an *aggregate* rather than a *group* to indicate that even the close physical proximity of the family gives no assurance that mother, father, grandparents, and children form a *group* wherein communication can take place with total or near total openness and honesty.

The simplest way to illustrate differences between *aggregate* and *group* appears in Figure 1. Here, the members interact, but the *aggregate* tone is more formal, more abstract, more guarded than that of the *group*. In the *aggregate*, members remain in protective boxes, keeping their feelings hidden most of the time. In the *group*, members are much more free to express feelings

AGGREGATE                    GROUP

Figure 1. Aggregate—Group

as well as thoughts. Less fear and judging of others occur in a group because its members cut through ritualized games that people learn to play with each other in order to avoid open expression of feeling.[2]

Not included in Figure 1, but developed throughout the book are the transitional stages in moving from aggregate to group. These stages include gathering information about others, sharing some of one's own, spending time together developing and testing what will be acceptable and appropriate behavior in this particular group (norms), trying out the expression of positive and negative feelings, and finding group support to relax and be oneself without the constant necessity to be on guard against judgment and attack.

Both the class with its teacher and the family with its father have every opportunity to move from aggregate to group status, and both usually move at least part of the way since they spend a great deal of time together and interact at least on formal levels. Yet even mother and father, together in the physical intimacies of marriage, sharing the joys and sorrows of raising a family, too often withhold feelings from each other or block expression of one partner's feelings. Picture a married couple, each grown uncertain of each other's love, each wanting to ask, coming together determined to find out, and ending up arguing about who should take out the garbage. Though this cartoon has its humorous aspects, it also contains overtones of sadness and frustration. Why in the world cannot people just sit down and share their feelings? The simple answer is that they have never learned· to interact in honesty without hurting or getting hurt. In addition, they *have* learned (you and I have learned) to avoid open expression of feelings and to play games. These games are often played with such skill that we forget that they are games and become, ourselves, dishonest and inauthentic.[3]

Man has taken great strides in understanding and developing ways to deal with his physical world in order to improve his lot.

---

[2] For a sometimes humorous, but psychologically based, treatment of devious human interaction, see Eric L. Berne, *Games People Play, The Psychology of Human Relationships* (New York: Grove Press, 1964).

[3] For good treatments of personal authenticity see Thomas A. Harris, *I'm OK—You're OK* (New York: Harper and Row, Publishers, 1969), and Sydney M. Jourard, *The Transparent Self* (Princeton, N.J.: D. Van Nostrand, 1964).

His machines and technologies have freed him enough in the twentieth century so that he can now begin to focus on problems of his interpersonal social and emotional world. He can now take time to raise questions about being human and search for authentic and anti-alienating contact with his fellows. As he once developed schools and teachers to instruct his young in matters of literacy, politics, economics, professions, and occupations, he is now in the process of directing schools and teachers to instruct also in matters of *affective* importance. This book, with its emphasis on helping aggregates mature into groups, is concerned directly with *affect education*.

While affect education is a serious, practical consideration in current educational thinking,[4] it will not come on the scene without some battles. It will be resisted by those who have spent long years learning to adapt to an aggregate existence; it will be viewed with alarm by those who feel that safety lies in keeping other people at a distance; but it will be fought for by those who know the joy of closeness without games, of emotional sharing without hurting, and of the expression of affection without self-consciousness. In the closing years of the twentieth century, we are moving toward human trust and interpersonal security as a viable alternative to lives lived in emotionally safe but lonely aggregate "boxes." The schools will be called upon to help. This, of course, means you.

## Teaching and Learning: Past

Sociologists describe education as a process through which the young of a society are inducted into the culture of the society. Inherent in this notion is the picture of an older and wiser authority controlling and shaping the behavior of an immature group of growing individuals. The degree of rigidity of such behavior control has depended upon the static or dynamic condition of the society at any given time. Thus in ancient societies frameworks of education, such as the Indian caste system and Plato's *Republic,* grew out of a felt need by elders to structure the present and future of their society in what seemed to them the best possible way.

Schooling (that part of education conducted in a formalized setting by specialists) began in the context of authority and the passing on by rote methods of universal truths that could not be questioned by young learners. The teacher knew, and that was why he was the teacher; the learner did not know, and that was why he was the learner. Communication between teachers and learners was one way at a time with the odds heavily weighted on the side of the teacher. First, the teacher would

[4] See George I. Brown, *Human Teaching for Human Learning* (New York: The Viking Press, 1971), and Gerald Weinstein and Mario D. Fantini, eds., *Toward Humanistic Education: A Curriculum of Affect* (New York: Praeger Publishers, 1970).

teach by lecturing and demonstrating; then, the learner would recite orally or on paper so that the teacher could determine whether understanding had taken place. Thus the now well-defined roles of teacher and student were developed. The teacher planned, introduced, developed, explained, illustrated, and summarized usually by oral means, though he might use drawings or models from time to time. The listening learner took notes, did individual thinking, and then demonstrated his success or failure to understand, or at least to recite, what he had been taught.

Motivation, concern, interest, need—all these were assumed. If the student lacked any of these, he was weeded out of the system. Proof of learning through test-taking was structured by the demand that the learner repeat the material in the teacher's terms without question. Any questioning or attempt to develop new knowledge was restricted to the mature person who had finished schooling. After years of enforced passive acceptance, however, the mature adult tended to be conditioned to the status quo.

Possibly because of his own conditioning, a man of the twentieth century would be disturbed by such a rote approach to schooling. It is clear, however, that such a world would be satisfying to many people who see the raising of questions as both threatening and difficult. Aldous Huxley, in *Brave New World*,[5] carries this notion of societal and personal security into the psychological setting of the modern world, and George Orwell, in *1984*,[6] goes further into the current notion of brainwashing to exact not only conformity but willing conformity from all citizens.

Even in the Renaissance, where inductive reasoning had taken hold, the experience of Galileo and others demonstrated the generality of violent resistance to change and to new ideas. In the nineteenth century, Semmelweis was driven insane by the refusal of his medical brethren to accept the suggestion that an examining doctor wash his hands. Such resistance came, at least in part, from the schooling practices of the time. Pasteur, with his talk about "little animals which no one could see,"

---

[5] Aldous Huxley, *Brave New World* (New York: Harper, 1946). See also by same author *Brave New World Revisited* (New York: Harper, 1958).
[6] George Orwell, *1984* (New York: Harcourt, 1949).

highlighted a changing climate in the acceptance of the new. Although he was initially resisted by higher authorities, he was eventually able to win his battle for acceptance in his own lifetime. During the past generation, Jonas Salk was able to put over a program for prevention of polio with only minimum resistance. During these centuries, schooling has slowly moved from being a simple mirror of society to acting as an agent for change or at least the acceptance of change.

## Teaching and Learning: Present

With the Renaissance came the beginnings of many things: the restructuring of social organizations within the society, the rise of a spirit of inductive inquiry into the physical—and later into the psychological—world, and the gradual development of leisure time for large numbers of the world population. The first of these changes put larger and larger percentages of available young people into schools; the second developed a generalized support for the growth of psychological investigation and support of its findings; the third gave more people time to think about, try out, and evaluate alternatives to the traditional wisdom.

In American schooling, this has led to challenges in a number of areas. Children are seldom currently thought of as little adults. Rather, they are perceived as growing organisms to be heard as well as seen. Even the most authoritarian American teacher must soften his approach or face the evaluation of his students in both of what he says and of him as a person. In response to what has been discovered about the needs of young people, an extensive cocurricular program has developed, and teachers in the regular curriculum areas have had to become more conscious of adaptive techniques to "reach" and to "motivate" their students.

Seats have been unscrewed from classroom floors (this is progress even though they may rarely be moved from their traditional places), the teacher's raised platform has all but disappeared, there is a permissive atmosphere (within certain rigid limits), and students are encouraged to question ideas in the now generally approved quest for "critical thinking." Teachers are expected to have good senses of humor, respect of and *for* students, well-developed habits of fair play, and approaches that are perceived as reasonable in students' terms. The modern American teacher must like his students and know them through permissive practices within the classroom, out-of-class encounters where possible, and consultation with parents, of permanent records, and with guidance counselors.

An ideal toward which today's teacher strives is to be a respected, genial buddy to his students without, of course, going "too far" and inviting behavior problems. He does not order; he requests. He stands at the front of the class in his section of the "egg-crate" school building before thirty youngsters seated in unscrewed, if unmoved, seats in rows one behind the other and waits for their acceptance of the fact that the period has begun. When they recover from their between-period gaiety and face expectantly to the front waiting for the performance called teaching to begin, he asks, "Would you open your books to page 28?" Rarely raised is the question as to what would happen if they replied, "No, we'd rather not."

Behind the apparently permissive atmosphere, however, lie many aspects of authoritarian control. Most grading of student effort includes evaluation of satisfactory conformity to the teacher's concept of good behavior, schools still use detention rooms, many teachers and principals hold to the belief in practice that the boy may be spoiled if the rod is spared, parents are frequently called in to account for the deviance of their offspring, and suspension and expulsion are always possible if all else seems to fail to bring a student into line with the expectations of a particular school. And these expectations may extend from behavior to appearance. A perfectly docile boy with long hair or a quiet girl with a very short skirt may find great pressure being applied by teachers and administrators to put an end to such flouting of the norms of their elders.

In the classroom, youngsters may flout, they may rebel, they may retreat into silence, they may smilingly conform, *but rarely do they have an opportunity to face the problems of intergenerational conflict squarely and to learn more constructive ways of handling it.*[7] Despite this, of course, some do learn to be self-directing and to cope with problems of authority. Many

---

[7] In some American high schools young blacks and whites occupy exclusive "territories" in an uneasy truce while their social studies teachers "cover" the age of Jackson.

others, however, go on struggling throughout their later marital and occupational encounters. It becomes more apparent each year that learning to deal creatively with oneself and others is a need at least as pressing as that of coping with the 3 R's. Clever writing alone does not explain the great popularity of Berne's book on the lack of authenticity in adult interaction.[8]

Teachers are beginning slowly to understand that any group setting is packed with human relations needs that have to be met before people can get on with the learning of subject matter. Large numbers of students find the traditional classroom actively harmful to their self-images day after day. Many withdraw physically and become dropout statistics; much larger numbers stay physically while withdrawing psychologically. Still others do not withdraw, but learn to play the highly sophisticated game of teachers and students much in the same way that they role-played cops and robbers at earlier ages. Their real world of personal meaning, where they can authentically play themselves, usually exists *outside* the classroom.

These students have intercommunication problems, and their teachers should be experts in communication. Unfortunately, this facet of teacher preparation has been almost totally ignored until quite recently. Teachers should be—and are to some extent—scholars in their subject disciplines. But teaching is not accomplished by the teachers demonstrating to their students how learned they, the teachers, are. Teaching is accomplished only when learners learn, retain what they learn, and develop both the urge to use their learning in later situations and some methodology for putting learnings to work. If one accepts these criteria, even what seems to be successful learning can be questioned. For example, the preservice teacher who gets an "A" in psychology and then goes into a class behaving as if he had never studied the subject can be said by his professor who granted the "A" to have learned the subject. But if he does not use his learnings or even think of them in an actual human situation, one might question the value of his having taken such a course in the first place. One answer could be that in many of his college classes, the teacher himself was playing the game of teachers and students.

[8] Berne, *Games People Play*.

In order to examine current notions of what teaching and learning is, a look at concepts now accepted in psychology and education is helpful. There is, of course, no guarantee that these notions have been or are being used. If they are not, it may be the ineffective way in which the teacher himself learned them—including the fact that while he may accept some or all, he may not know how to implement them.

The following list is illustrative rather than exhaustive. The student is encouraged to read more deeply in the field and to develop his own basic set of concepts to guide his teaching.

1. Learners (and teachers) bring with them to the classroom a cluster of understandings, skills, appreciations, attitudes, and feelings that have personal meaning to them and are in effect the sum of their reactions to previous stimuli.

2. Learners (and teachers) are individually different in many ways even when ability grouped.

3. Learners (and teachers) have developed concepts of self, which directly affect their behavior.

4. Learning may be defined as a change in behavior.

5. Learning requires activity on the part of the learner. He should not be passive.

6. Learners ultimately learn what they actively desire to learn; they do not learn what they do not accept or come to accept as meaningful and useful.

7. Learning is enhanced when learners accept responsibility for their own learning.

8. Learning is directly influenced by physical and social environment.

9. Learning is deepened when the learning situation provides opportunity for applying learnings in as realistic a situation as is feasible.

10. Learners are more highly motivated when they understand and accept the purposes of the learning situation than when they do not.

11. Learners are motivated by success experiences.

12. Learners tend to be motivated by teacher acceptance.

13. Learners are motivated when they can associate new learnings with previous learnings.

14. Learners are motivated when they can see the usefulness of the learning in their own personal terms.

Number one (what teachers and learners bring to the classroom) refers to what John Dewey wrote concerning the "Whole Child" and what the present author calls the "Whole Teacher." These are the hidden ingredients of the interaction process. While they affect everything that goes on in the class, they are usually ignored since the traditional rules of the "teacher and students game" state that everyone must "get down to business" and start covering the ground even before students and teacher develop any personal relationships.

Number two (individual differences) has become a cliché which everyone recognizes like Mark Twain's weather, but which they often fail to deal with. Again, much of the problem here is caused by the almost hysterical urge on the part of many teachers not to waste time. The result of such an urge can be a set style and approach to all learners. The possible waste of individual students' time with this approach apparently does not cause the same high level of concern on the part of the teacher.

Number three (self-concept), like one and two, is often ignored because teachers have not, themselves, received affect education. Their ignorance can harm student self-concepts. Many teachers, kindly and considerate in other contexts, can be heard to say to visitors (often within hearing range of lower ability grouped students), "These are the dummies. You really should come around during the sixth period and see my good class." Sometimes the most effective learning that a student does is to develop clearly the notion that he is stupid, dirty, and undesirable.

Number four (learning as change in behavior) relates to outcomes of the classroom experience. It usually refers to increased ability to deal intelligently with the subject matter and to be able to apply it where relevant. Students, of course, may learn things that the teacher *does not intend,* such as how to flatter superiors and to cheat on tests. It also deals with attitude development. Sinclair Lewis' Babbitt[9] bragged that his college learn-

─────────────

[9] Sinclair Lewis, *Babbitt* (New York: Harcourt, 1950).

ings had never touched him. In *The Corn Is Green*,[10] on the other hand, a teacher who was not satisfied with merely presenting material made a successful effort to reach a young man who had not been profiting from his learning before his encounter with her. The implication seems to be that the teacher must reach each student before he can begin to teach him. A few teachers just do not care, but others who do are blocked by not knowing *how* to reach students.

Numbers five through fourteen deal directly with the students "buying into" the teaching-learning process. For an optimal educational experience, the teacher must help the student to be active intellectually; to desire to learn; to accept the instructional purpose; to feel immediate success and the possibility of further success; to fulfill his social needs of acceptance, achievement, and affection; and to see "something in it for him" in terms of both immediate and future usefulness of the learning.

A big job? Of course it is. And it requires the development of usable concepts by the teacher. Too often, in the history of teacher education, students have filed such data as these fourteen statements away on their mental shelves as nice, hazy, idealistic things to put into practice when and if they ever get around to them. Thus there has existed, and still exists, a frustrating gap between theory and practice. More effective and more truly professional education will occur only when the teacher sees concepts such as these as stark realities that will not disappear even if one pretends they do not exist. They *do* exist, and they are vital ingredients of schooling that need to take their proper place alongside the equally necessary teacher expertise in subject matter.


## Teaching and Learning: Future

Relevance and reality are the touchstones of the education of the future. From pseudoscholarship, American schools are slowly swinging their values toward teaching and learning for present and future living. All the really good things of the past will doubtless survive, but they will have to continue to prove them-

[10] Emlyn Williams, *The Corn Is Green* (New York: Random House, 1941).

selves. To support a vaguely stated upholding of standards, we have for far too long studied Silas Marner, parts of speech, and what Arnold Toynbee has called the "one damn thing after another" approach to history. Scientific method—long given lip service praise in the schools—calls for questioning and proof. It is high time that it be made available to students so that they, as well as teachers and parents, can raise questions and demand proof concerning the content and method of their education.

Referring to *entropy*—the tendency of an organism to wear out and come to a stop—and pointing up the danger of this process happening in our schools, Postman and Weingartner ask: "What is the necessary business of the schools? To create eager consumers? To transmit the dead ideas, values, metaphors, and information of (the past) . . . ? To create smoothly functioning bureaucrats? *These* aims . . . undermine our chances of surviving as a viable, democratic society. . . . We would like to see the schools go into the anti-entropy business."[11] And what is *anti-entropy*? They go on to say: "We have been insisting that the new education is new, not because it offers more of anything, but because it enters into an entirely new 'business': fundamentally, the crap-detecting and relevance business."[12]

Sounds irreverent and critical, you say? But the schools are not religious institutions and are certainly not beyond criticism. Besides, who would rush to the barricades to defend "crap"? Better, as these authors advocate, help students to detect crap and get rid of it rather than honor it.

In *Education and Ecstasy*, Leonard raised questions about hidden goals of education focused on conditioning students to competition, acquisition, aggression, and conformity. He said: "Schools and colleges have until now . . . served a society that needed reliable, predictable, human components. Appropriately enough, they spent overwhelming amounts of time and energy ironing out those human impulses and capabilities that seemed errant. . . . Perhaps half of all learning ability was squelched in the earliest elementary grades, where children found out that there exist predetermined and unyielding 'right answers' for everything; that following instructions is what really counts;

[11] Neil Postman and Charles Weingartner, *Teaching as a Subversive Activity* (New York: Delacorte Press, 1969), p. 15.
[12] Ibid., p. 82.

and, most surprisingly, that the whole business of education is mostly dull and painful."[13]

Moving from this description of education for past societal needs (Riesman's inner-directed man[14]), Leonard sees a different direction for the future (Riesman's autonomous man): "Where the actions of one can drastically affect the lives of others far distant, it will be crucially important that each person master the skill of feeling what others feel. . . . One of the first tasks of education, then, is to return man to himself; to encourage rather than stifle awareness; to educate the emotions, the senses, the so-called autonomic systems; to help people become truly responsive and therefore truly responsible."[15]

A number of authors support Leonard's (and the present author's) call for educating the emotions. To dip into a few to get the flavor of what is being said, there is Brown: "Everywhere we hear cries that education is 'irrelevant.' Millions of American children find that our system doesn't work for them: they fail in it, they drop out, they protest, or they are thrown out. Surely, there are many reasons for discontent with the present educational system, and surely the reasons for this discontent will have to be attacked in a great variety of ways. But one cannot help thinking that an underlying reason for this discontent is the schools' lack of attention to the total human needs of their students: specifically their emotional . . . needs."[16] He goes on to say: "Attempts at communication solely on a rational level are bound to fail when the issues involved have personal relevance for the participants. Personal relevance connotes an affective dimension; people feel and value as well as think about the position they hold. Denying or ignoring the existence of feelings in communication is like building a house without a foundation or framework."[17] Yet many teachers energetically deny

[13] George B. Leonard, *Education and Ecstasy* (New York: Dell Publishing Co., Inc., 1969), p. 120.
[14] Riesman developed the notions of the tradition-directed man, the inner-directed man, and the other-directed man. Above the cultural manipulation of all three is the autonomous man. David Riesman, *The Lonely Crowd* (New Haven: Yale University Press, 1950).
[15] Leonard, *Education and Ecstasy*, p. 127.
[16] George I. Brown, *Human Teaching for Human Learning* (New York: The Viking Press, 1971), pp. xv-xvi.
[17] Ibid., p. 6.

that the expression of personal feeling has any place in the classroom. In this, perhaps, one reason why so many accuse the schools of being irrelevant? Is it easier to jabber on about Columbus and Washington than to face each other, person to person, and decide what we would really like to be doing with our time in this classroom?

In a book significantly titled, *A Curriculum of Affect*, Weinstein and Fantini comment that *"Significant contact with pupils is most effectively established and maintained when the content and method of instruction have an affective basis.* That is, if educators are able to discover the feelings, fears, and wishes that move pupils emotionally they can more effectively engage pupils from any background. . . ."[18]

Rogers sees a changing environment demanding a changed education: "Teaching and the imparting of knowledge make sense in an unchanging environment. This is why it has been an unquestioned function for centuries. But if there is one truth about modern man, it is that he lives in an environment which is *continually changing.* . . . We are . . . faced with an entirely new situation in education where the goal of education, if we are to survive, is the *facilitation of change and learning.* . . . We possess a very considerable knowledge of the conditions which encourage self-initiated, significant, experiential, 'gut-level' learning by the whole person. We do not frequently see these conditions put into effect because they mean a real revolution in our approach to education and revolutions are not for the timid."[19]

Clark and Kadis bring the whole business into the classroom, citing actual teacher-student behavior: ". . . the general idea is that feelings are related to learning, and only when we know more about them can we cope with them in a learning context. A teacher, as the central member of the class, can demonstrate how to identify and show feelings. A middle-aged wife and mother recently went back to school and became a teacher. During her first year she worried about how often she yelled at some of her second-graders—for instance, Gregory, who was usually out of his seat and loudly involved with a classmate when there was a need for relative quiet. One day she

[18] Gerald Weinstein and Mario D. Fantini, *Toward Humanistic Education: A Curriculum of Affect* (New York: Praeger Publishers, 1971), p. 10.
[19] Carl R. Rogers, *Freedom to Learn* (Columbus, Ohio: Charles E. Merrill Publishing Co., 1969), pp. 104-105.

asked him to pass the wastebasket, then became involved in a problem with several other children. Catching sight of him out of the corner of her eye, she said sharply, 'Gregory, get back to your seat this instant!!!' He returned to his seat, but said plaintively, 'You told me to pass the wastebasket.' Her face registered dismay. 'I'm terribly sorry, Gregory,' she said, 'I apologize. I got so involved with Susan and Geraldine that I forgot. You must be furious with me!' The boy smiled and said, 'I like you because when you do something wrong, you say you're sorry.' Some interesting things happened in those few moments. The teacher owned up to some of her own feelings and Gregory owned up to some of his. It is not difficult to believe this honesty will affect the teacher-student relationship which will, in turn, affect Gregory's receptiveness to school learning."[20]

Such books as those quoted from above and others now in print or in preparation present a thrilling—and, to many of us, a somewhat threatening—challenge to the status quo. They call for a more authentic teacher who will take more personal risks in a more personally involved classroom role. This is a more viable approach to the enormous problems of contemporary schooling than the teacher as detached subject-matter expert. It is the position of this author, however, that mere calling for radical change is bound to fail. What is needed, in addition to pointing out a new direction, is a way, or ways, that we, as teachers, can learn to operate in a more humanistic fashion without too much threat to ourselves as persons or to the knowledge, understandings, and skills we are charged to impart to our learners. Humanistic teaching and affect education does not call for the abandonment of present curriculum content—except for some of the "crap" we have come to value—but rather asks us to reexamine it in terms of its relevance. And, just as important as this, we must come to view methodology more on equal terms with content. McLuhan points up this equality nicely when he states that the medium is the message.[21] What he is saying, in essence, is that when knowledge is transmitted, the learner learns from the transmission experience as well as from what is being transmitted.

[20] Donald H. Clark and Asya L. Kadis, *Humanistic Teaching* (Columbus, Ohio: Charles E. Merrill Publishing Co., 1971), pp. 50-51.
[21] Marshall McLuhan and Quentin Fiore, *The Medium Is the Massage* (New York: Bantam Books, Inc., 1970).

All stages of learning ultimately form a composite within the individual learner. For purposes of discussion, however, it is helpful to analyze the process stage by stage in order to deal separately with each component. It should be recognized, of course, that any such analysis must refer to a particular definition of learning. The analysis here infers a certain way of viewing learning that has been suggested by the findings in the social psychology of education for over a generation.

Components of learning within the concept used in this book would include: (1) readiness activities; (2) organizational cognitive processes; (3) feedback of intellectual and emotional response; (4) adjustive cognitive processes; (5) guided application; (6) valuing and internalizing; and (7) summarizing feedback.

One of the first things a class and its teacher will do in the future (and good learning experiences of the past and present have shown awareness of this necessity) will be to carry on activities that will cut through *over*formal, distrustful relationships. The whole child *and* the whole teacher come into the classroom. Each has individual values, attitudes, and characteristic ways of behaving and of perceiving others. As they get to know each other, it becomes less necessary for them to employ irritating behaviors, and even the behaviors themselves become less irritating. When we *know* Charlie or Patricia, we are much more accepting of their behavior. This, in turn, makes it less necessary for us to change their behavior so that they can become more like us. It might be much more helpful to all concerned if they became more authentically *like themselves.* [22]

---

[22] *Authenticity* is used here in the sense of being spontaneously frank about your feelings in your relations with others. The non-authentic teacher when threatened by two whispering students will use sarcasm or force to stop the threat. The authentic teacher will tell the students, in the class setting, that he feels uncomfortable because they are talking. This second behavior will bring the conflict out into the open where it can be resolved. The first behavior only increases both teacher and student frustration.

On page 153 of *The Transparent Self* Sidney M. Jourard says, "This entire book can be regarded as an invitation to 'authentic being.' Authentic being means being oneself honestly, in one's relations with his fellows. It means taking the first step at dropping pretense, defenses, and duplicity. It means an end to 'playing it cool,' an end to using one's behavior as a gambit designed to disarm the other fellow, to get him to reveal himself *before* you disclose yourself to him."

Normal "entry activity" for all of us, as a group (class) begins, is to test for rules and boundaries. None of us can really relax and be ourselves until we learn, in our own terms, just what is expected of us and how people get treated in this new situation. In most cases, we attempt to learn the rules from observing others. Only forceful, dominating personalities attempt personally to build the norms of the group in its initial moves. In the classroom, the age and authority difference between teacher and students usually puts the teacher, at least in the beginning stages, in the position of norm setter. But readiness activities could provide the opportunity *and the responsibility* of norm setting for the students as well as for the teacher. This process of sharing is a difficult one because it has not been a norm in traditional classroom interaction and because both teachers and students have locked themselves into stereotyped roles. A group-centered norm will not appear just because the teacher smiles and says, "Let's plan our learning experience together." To overcome years of dependency conditioning (and this includes the teacher), the group will have to learn first how people work together. Only then can they effectively plan together.

Such initial learning, while difficult, will pay spectacular dividends as the aggregate of individuals begins to become a cohesive group of learners. Once the interaction pattern has been established so that rules of the game and expectations of teacher and students are known, the process of cognitive growth can go on in a more relaxed and enthusiastic atmosphere with less need for dominating or withdrawal behavior. At this point, the group is really ready to organize itself for learning and carrying out inquiry into the discipline under consideration in this particular class.

The third step (feedback) would include various ways of checking and testing the group norms. Have feelings changed? Is everyone participating freely? Do we need to modify the norms, or do we have to admit that they never were really accepted by all members? How can we improve the social-emotional climate of the group?

Integrated with this feedback would be a check on the understanding of facts, concepts, skills, and other learnings. Have we learned what we set out to learn? What do we have to do now? Can we go ahead or do we have to relearn some material? How can we use what we have done to go further? What avenues of inquiry have been opened?

Step four (adjustive cognitive processes) is an outgrowth of step three, and it consists of actions taken in response to the questions raised by the feedback. The learning group has now progressed a fair distance on the road to becoming a mature, self-directing, self-correcting set of individuals. Dependence on the teacher as initiator, lecturer, and sole evaluator has been somewhat lessened, and students are reacting to the responsibility for making the learning a successful experience. Dealing with the data from the feedback process, they have become more able to cooperate with the teacher in planning and carrying out an application experience where they can put their learnings to a test. In arriving at this point, they are able to benefit more fully from the teacher's knowledge and talents. And he himself can play the professional role of intellectual guide and mentor less distracted by the baby-sitting chores that result from a noncohesive group where the teacher and the students find themselves on opposing sides of an emotional game whose very existence is denied while so-called teaching goes on.

While the application experience of step five proceeds, the sixth step of valuing and internalizing keeps pace. The latter step involves student evaluation of the experience in his own terms—a personal involvement in deciding what is important to him, what can be used, what further learnings are necessary. The testing and reporting process is put in more proper perspective. Learning, evaluating, and using the evaluations for further learning replace the anti-intellectual question, "What mark did I get?" The student begins to take control and responsibility for self-evaluation both in this class and beyond. His personal values are brought into play and reinforced or modified as he is given opportunity to see personal meaning in his educational process.

To be consistent with the other components, summarizing feedback (step seven) should be provided following both short-range and long-range points of the teaching-learning process. Such feedback should be student-teacher planned evaluations of learning experiences, and enough time should be provided to make them meaningful reinforcements of previous learnings.

Contrast this to traditional testing carried on solely by the teacher, taking place through final examinations, and using results only to support a grade on a piece of paper. For students, such an experience is one of regurgitating rather than of learning. When these "finals" are given to students a second time six weeks later and a third time six months later to determine student retention of learning, the results are usually discouraging. If, however, summarizing feedback is planned and used by both students and teacher to evaluate, reinforce, and test relevance and meaning of the learning, retention should be at a maximum.

## Where Are We Now?

In the class where you are a student reading this book (or in the class where you are a teacher) is there an opportunity to deal with the material presented thus far? Can students discuss points made, or are they looking to the teacher to tell them what they have read? Is he or she stepping into this dominating role or is the discussion ball being thrown back to the students? What is the climate of feeling in your class? What are its norms of behavior? Who set them? How are they tested? Where will you go from here? Will your experience in this class have personal meaning for your future? What have you done to help your teacher to be a better teacher? Is he—in your eyes—a human being or just a convenient scapegoat for your own lack of interest, motivation, creativity, imagination, initiative, or energy?

## Summary

What has this chapter been about? It began with the notion of family and schooling *aggregates* having the potential to become *groups*. Then it noted some of education's pressing current problems and some of the current alternatives to traditional notions as to what schooling should be about. Finally, psychological and methodological components of teaching and learning were stated and elaborated to begin building a base for the presentation of a classroom interaction theory in Chapter 2.

The once revolutionary idea that education should be for all has caught up with American schools almost before they were ready. Since they had been in the college preparation business for such a long time, their readiness to deal with other types of students was not highly developed. Failures to reach the non-college bound are easily documented by dropout statistics. Since, in America, the teenage dropout has literally no place to go but the street corner, his leaving the school is a biting criticism. But, while this is a problem, the case of the psychological dropout, less easily documented, should give the highly subject-centered teacher much to think about.

Yet, mere thinking will not solve problems. The traditionally educated teacher has rarely been taught effectively to teach *people*. He, and his professors, have concentrated on the learning of the subject often at the expense of the development of methodology in teaching it. Even the currently new ideas in schooling practices contain little that relates directly to what the teacher does when he is teaching. Much has been written about the organization of team teaching, but little exists that details the how of the practice. If current teaching leaves much to be desired, the creation of teams will not, in itself, improve the situation. It is time that new approaches to *interaction* in the classroom were developed and tested. The material in this book should provide at least a small step in this direction.

Past teaching has too often consisted of authoritarian *telling* by the teacher to a rigidly controlled over-conforming captive audience. Present teaching is moving toward more student involvement and less rigid teacher control. Future teachers will do less telling as a one-way process. They will instead focus on teacher-student and student-student interaction and its improvement in both the cognitive and affective domains. Such a focus should result in more freedom, more responsibility, and more learning for all members of the classroom group including the teacher himself.

# The Teacher and the Class:
## *A Theoretical Framework for Interaction*

In Chapter 1, the outlines of the book were drawn in broad strokes. It is time to sketch in the details before proceeding to actual teaching operations. Chapter 1 is an overview of teaching, and Chapter 2 is the theory underlying a certain approach to teaching. The remaining chapters will illustrate this approach.

### The Theory

Because interaction is at the base of the material presented here, and because it is a frequently misunderstood term, a definition at this point is in order.

Human confrontation and communication (meeting and speaking) is a fascinating interplay of subtle assumptions and meanings that most people learn to deal with in a more or less effective fashion. Difficulties arise when meanings are not clarified or when assumptions are not checked. Such clarifying and checking, however, is not always an easy matter. How, for example, can a sixth-grade boy go about asking his teacher whether or not he really meant to be sarcastic?

There is a communication joke that becomes more profound as one speculates about the hidden meanings and assumptions implied. It involves two psychologists who meet in the lobby of a hotel after breakfast. "Good morning," says Dr. Brown. "I wonder what he meant by that," thinks Dr. Green.

Green's question may be provoked by something perceived in Brown's behavior, or it may be merely that Green is making an unfounded assumption that a hidden meaning exists. If he follows the pattern of most people, however, he will never ask his question aloud except possibly later to a third person. This failure to check, in itself, serves to cloud further communication between the two men, but an even more serious problem can arise. Green may try to get an answer from Brown without actually asking the question. Getting further verbal and non-verbal responses from Brown, he may build on his original assumption that Brown was being unfriendly or mocking or whatever. If Green can convince himself that his assumption is correct (notice that he never really checks it directly), he may take retaliatory action by being nasty to or by ignoring Brown. Meanwhile, Brown may not have felt anything but good will toward Green and be puzzled by his nasty response. This puzzlement can turn to anger on Brown's part and a feeling that good will is wasted on the likes of people like Green. Following the unfortunate human habit of failing to check on assumptions, he will probably not ask Green what the trouble is. Instead, Brown may, himself, become nasty, thus assuring Green that he was correct in his original assumption.

In the classroom, a similar miscommunication may occur between teacher and student, and the presence of the other members of the class usually makes things worse. Using the pattern of *Assumption, Intent, Message, Reception,* the interchange might go like this:

| *Johnny* | *Message* |
|---|---|
| *Assumption:* The teacher appreciates honesty in student responses. He has made this statement in class. | |
| *Intent:* I'll try telling him what I really think about Beethoven. Maybe he can help me to understand the music. (I'll also show the class that I'm not a square.) | "Mr. Williams, I can't get with this Beethoven character. He doesn't send me anywhere." |

## Teacher

*Reception:* I really want students to respond and respond honestly, especially Johnny. I feel good that he has finally spoken.

*Assumption:* He likes and trusts me. He has a good sense of humor. He is familiar with the notion of long hair in connection with classical music.

*Intent:* I'll make a joke to show him and the class that I'm not just an old fuddy duddy. This will bring us closer and encourage him toward more class participation.

"Johnny, with your long hair I thought you'd be the first person in the class to appreciate classical music."

## Johnny

*Reception:* Oh, oh. What's happening here? The class laughed, and I looked like a fool. I feel uncomfortable and a little fearful. That's what I get for trying to play the game straight.

*Assumption:* Mr. Williams doesn't really want honesty. Also, he doesn't like me or the way I wear my hair. Also, he is a sarcastic so-and-so.

*Intent:* I'll show him. He can't push me around and get away with it. Also, I'll regain my leadership of the class. They won't laugh again.

"Well, Mr. Williams, only squares from squaresville like that kind of garbage. Nobody who was a real man would waste his time listening to it. I don't know why we have to study this junk anyway."

## Teacher

*Reception:* That hurt. He slams the subject just when I have most of the kids motivated. He raises the old questions of the virility of male music teachers. And just when I

thought he was coming a-
round and getting interested.

*Assumption:* Johnny is just a
nasty, fresh boy. You can't
treat his kind with decency—
all he understands is force. He
is ignorant, he doesn't like me,
and he is turning the class
against me and the subject.

*Intent:* I will straighten him out.
He must not get away with
insolence. It is bad for discipline. I will show him who is
boss here.

"We will have no more of that
sort of talk, young man. If you
can't appreciate good music, the
least you can do is to keep quiet
and not parade your ignorance.
*(To class)* Now, the next record
we will hear is . . ."

### Johnny

*Reception:* I know I'm not so
bright, but it hurts to have
the teacher hit me over the
head with it.

*Assumption:* Mr. Williams is really
a fraud. He puts on a nice act,
but he's really a fink just like
most teachers. I tried to be
honest, and now he's really
out to get me.

*Intent:* I'll keep my mouth shut
from now on, but I won't pay
any attention to this music
junk. It's sort of too bad. I'd
sort of like to know more
about it, but that's out now.
I'll show that so-and-so.

In analyzing the interchange above, several things should
be noted:

1. This is a case of blocked interaction. What will follow with
   the class will not be interaction but a series of one-way
   actions.
2. Interaction includes feelings and perceptions in addition to
   messages.

3. Interaction occurs only when messages and assumptions of the sender's intent are clarified.

4. Socialization norms in the American society act against such clarification. Rarely do we check our assumptions directly even with close friends.

5. People often react defensively to words without considering the person saying them. (Johnny was quick to take offense without considering that Mr. Williams might possibly have meant his statement as a joke and might be clumsy in expressing himself. Mr. Williams was quick to form a judgment of Johnny without considering that the laughter of the class might have hurt Johnny's feelings and that his need for peer status was unusually strong.)

6. Effective interaction is difficult before people form relationships and check out some of their initial assumptions about each other. (If Johnny had confidence in Mr. Williams' generally good intentions, he would not have reacted so rapidly without giving the teacher the benefit of the doubt.)

7. A group situation makes initially difficult interaction even more so. (It was the laughter of the class that hastened Johnny's defensive reaction. It was the thought of the bad effect on the class that helped Mr. Williams decide to put Johnny in his place in an authoritarian manner. And the class itself undoubtedly had varied individual reactions to the interchange that would affect *their* behavior toward Mr. Williams and Johnny in the future.)

Interaction, then, is a process of communication between two or more people where both the linguistic meaning and the emotional response are mutually clarified whenever clarification seems necessary. As is noted in number 6 above, the development of relationships is helpful to effective interaction. This suggests that less need for clarification becomes necessary as more meaningful relationships are formed. With close friends, for example, we do not have to be constantly on guard against misunderstanding. We say that our friends *understand us*, by which we mean that they do not misinterpret our intent even when our language is clumsy. Also, we *understand them*, by which we mean that we trust them and feel that their intent is to be helpful and supportive.

Some of the determinants of interactive situations may be illustrated as follows: Person A, finding himself in a social situation, wishes to communicate with person B. Before codifying his message, however, he passes his thoughts through a number of personal "screens." In such screening, he asks himself questions about:

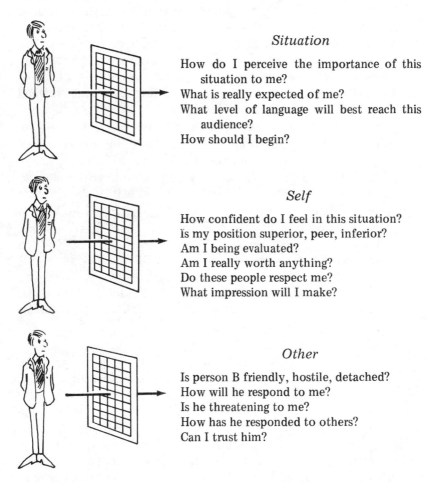

### Situation

How do I perceive the importance of this situation to me?

What is really expected of me?

What level of language will best reach this audience?

How should I begin?

### Self

How confident do I feel in this situation?

Is my position superior, peer, inferior?

Am I being evaluated?

Am I really worth anything?

Do these people respect me?

What impression will I make?

### Other

Is person B friendly, hostile, detached?

How will he respond to me?

Is he threatening to me?

How has he responded to others?

Can I trust him?

When A attempts to communicate with B, his attempt and his feelings about it are somewhat influenced, in a group situation, by persons C, D, E, F, G, and H. All of these impressions may finally inhibit him to the point of silence even though he wants to say something. He may feel that the risk involved in speaking is too great for him to overcome.

If and when he does speak to B, B and the others receive the message through *their* perceptual screens as in Figure 2. B's reply is filtered through *his* screens and comes back to A through A's incoming screens. In addition to B's reply, of course, A also receives verbal or nonverbal messages from the other members of the group (the laughter of the class while Johnny was speaking to Mr. Williams). All of these messages, some quite problematical and unclear, must be decoded by A before he can make a decision to speak again or to remain silent.

In the interaction process, *when it is not blocked*, the people involved get a chance to check on and clarify their initial perceptions. As person A sends his message, observes reactions of others, and receives replies, his initial perceptions may change. He may have thought, for example, that no one would be interested in what he had to say. If he perceives, after speaking, that they *are* interested, he will be reinforced and more able to send out further messages. He may also be able to differentiate the cognitive and emotional components of his message. His listeners may indicate interest, but lack of cognitive understanding. The perceived interest will prompt A to further efforts to make

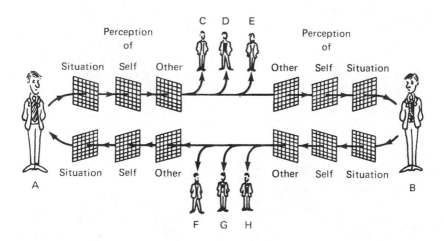

Figure 2. Perceptual Screens in Group Interaction

himself cognitively clear. Side effects are also numbered in the interactions. Person G, for example, may have been inhibited, but seeing the success of A, may be prompted to try a message of his own.

The notion of interaction, then, includes both emotional and cognitive communication. What is too often ignored in classroom operation is the emotional component. Until a person is at ease (gets to *know* the others), he will not be able to concentrate fully on the cognitive component of the communication process. If person A speaks to B, and D laughs, followed by a sarcastic reply from B, then A may be less inclined to speak again. The sensitive teacher will help students to deal helpfully with each other; the insensitive teacher will merely wonder why A has become so quiet and urge him to speak up.

Sensitivity and *knowing each other* can be developed in the classroom, and its value to the learning of the subject is great.[1] Such conditions by no means suggest that everyone tiptoe about the classroom, fearful of expressing any negative feelings. Rather, it opens the way for dealing with negative reactions in a helpful manner. After all, friends often disagree, but they remain friends. Where interaction is blocked, people treat each other in a formal, ritualistic manner or avoid contact altogether. Where it is unblocked, people get to know each other, there is less need for careful screening, and problems that do occur are dealt with. In a cohesive group, the laughter of D and the sarcastic reply of B would be clarified and dealt with there and then. Others would come in to support A and to mediate between A and B. There would also be opportunity for D to clarify the meaning of his laughter. The point is that, even under difficult conditions, the interaction would not stop, and people would not keep their reactions hidden. They would, instead, bring out the feelings and deal with them before going on.

---

[1] For one of the classics in classroom student-centered teaching see Nathaniel Cantor, *The Dynamics of Learning* (Buffalo, N.Y.: Foster and Stewart, 1946). For adaptations of nondirective counseling in the classroom setting see Carl R. Rogers, *Client-Centered Therapy* (Boston: Houghton Mifflin, 1965), Chapter 9, "Student-Centered Teaching," pp. 384-428. For a probing look at the learning of improved group membership behavior see Matthew B. Miles, *Learning to Work in Groups* (New York: Bureau of Publications, Teachers College, Columbia University, 1959).

There seem to be two important reasons for working to produce a cohesive group (getting to know, trust, and feel for each other).

First, people tend to work toward their potential in a warm, supportive setting where they can concentrate on learning without too much worry about their social needs. While learning may take place in a cold, formal setting, it is not often very efficient in terms of depth or retention. Without group cohesion many children do not respond openly, and the teacher is forced to persuade, coax, or threaten to get student participation. A warmer, more informal setting does not magically make a fast learner out of a slow learner, but it gives more assurance that each student will be motivated to work up to his individual level of competence.[2]

Second, the building of a cohesive group, which is a challenging learning situation in itself, teaches students to be more self-directing, happier human beings. In actuality, the "Let's get down to business—no nonsense—be quiet and pay attention—we have to cover the ground" approach of many teachers is a self-defeating travesty of professional teaching. It is based on fearful inhibition that makes the teacher and the students less human than they might otherwise be. It is a request that students suspend all social needs (acceptance, achievement, affection) because these have nothing to do with *serious* class work. The stubborn fact remains that students cannot do such a thing even if they can be persuaded to try.

## Interaction

True interaction produces a cohesive classroom group where teacher and students share responsibility for the defining,

---

[2] People have always been able to learn facts and concepts without warmth, but they also learn to be remote. Since evidence is conflicting and behavioral outcomes of teaching are rarely measured, perhaps teachers need to experiment and test their objectives more than they do. As used here, warmth implies gentleness, respect, and consideration as opposed to harshness, domination, and disregard of needs and feelings. The teacher who defines warmth as a soupy permissiveness that demands no student effort or performance should check his own attitudes toward self and others.

carrying out, and evaluating of the learning experience. Set forth as an ideal, this sounds exciting and valuable; seen against the background of twenty-five to thirty youngsters in a typical school setting, the ideal seems a difficult one to reach. *And it is.* But the traditional alternative of maintaining an aggregate of noncommunicating individuals from September to June seems an even more difficult situation.

Creation of a group by a collection of individuals releases the creative potential of the total membership. The business of teaching and learning does not become easier (it is one of the most difficult of human enterprises), but the abrasive little problems of motivation and discipline largely disappear. The students unite with the teacher to get the job done, which is much more satisfying than the situation in which the teacher tries to do the whole thing all by himself.

Sound good? Fine. But how to accomplish it? As a first step there is need for a usable theory that details necessary conditions and sets ground rules for action.

## Building Blocks

In building a theory of interaction, it is necessary to deal with three basic factors: (1) the initial human situation, (2) subsequent behaviors, and (3) outcomes.

Watson[3] conceptualizes these ingredients of an input-output system as STRUCTURE—PROCESS—ATTITUDE. He sees the society as a whole made up of a number of social systems, each having its own generally accepted (by the people involved) STRUCTURE. This STRUCTURE determines the relative positions of persons within the system, and since each position implies the appropriate position behavior, those occupying each position (somewhat like chess pieces) know what they can (should) and cannot (should not) do as long as they are members of that particular group.

When individuals act (and they generally act according to the behavioral expectations that accompany each position), their

[3] These notions are explored in depth in Goodwin Watson, *Social Psychology: Issues and Insights* (Philadelphia: J. B. Lippincott, 1966), pp. 189-213.

actions make up the PROCESS of the system. The playing out of the PROCESS develops generalized ATTITUDES in the participants. Thus a father, acting in accord with the culturally determined STRUCTURE of the family, comes to feel that this is the natural way *all* fathers should act.

The family is the earliest social system experienced by most people. In American homes, the STRUCTURE of the family may include the father as breadwinner, the mother as housekeeper, the children as ornaments differentiated as to position by age and sex, and possibly one or more grandparents who may have relinquished their earlier supreme authority in the system and now are seen as burdens to be carried.

This STRUCTURE is diagrammed in Figure 3 with PROCESS indicated by relative size of symbols and direction of arrows. The father is supreme ruler, with mother subordinate and close, and grandfather subordinate and further removed. The children, also subordinate, tend to form a subsystem with the oldest as ruler.

In defining position behavior, it is assumed and accepted (a group norm) that father will make major decisions, that mother will act to support him, that grandfather will have little to say, that the sons will be obedient and submissive, and that

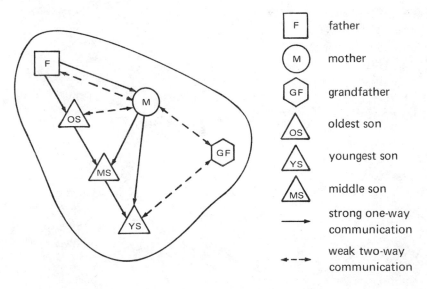

Figure 3. Social System: The Family

the oldest son will act like the father in minor decisions affecting the subsystem of sons that he directs.

In addition to behavioral norms, STRUCTURE would include spatial configuration and territories. Father and mother would occupy the largest bedroom, the oldest son would have his own room, the two remaining sons would share a room, and grandfather would sleep on a folding bed in the living room. All this territory occupation would flow with STRUCTURE, would develop individual and group activities, and would influence individual and group attitudes toward self and others.

While various members, from time to time, may resist the PROCESS, they accept the STRUCTURE because they know no other and assume that it is natural to mankind. Their ATTITUDES develop from their behavior, which itself has developed from the expectations surrounding the position they occupy. And these attitudes will have great persistence even when they go outside the family into other systems. Thus, the son of an authoritarian father may have difficulty relating to a permissive teacher.

Figure 4 suggests the same basic family situation existing in Figure 3, but with a different STRUCTURE. Here, the communication pattern brings people in on a more equal basis, with

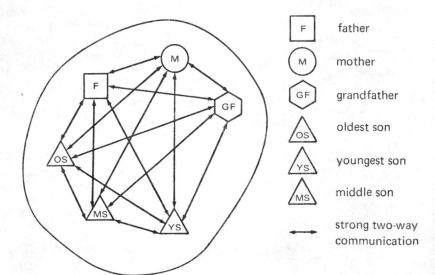

Figure 4. Social System: The Family

everyone sharing in major decisions though father and mother have somewhat more influence than grandfather, and the sons have least influence. In this STRUCTURE, the PROCESS demands more thought, responsibility, and self-direction from the participants, and the ATTITUDE outcomes are different. *These* children may have difficulty relating to an extremely authoritarian teacher, though they should tend to be more understanding and less judgmental because of their democratic upbringing.

## Structure, Process, and Attitude in the Classroom

Transferring this framework (SPA) to the classroom as a social system, as in Figure 5a, one can see the physical and psychological aspects of a traditional situation. Its STRUCTURE includes thirty students seated in rows facing the teacher, who has a larger desk and chair, stands at the front, and may, in some cases, have a raised platform on which to stand. He is, of course, generally bigger, older, and more knowledgeable in the given

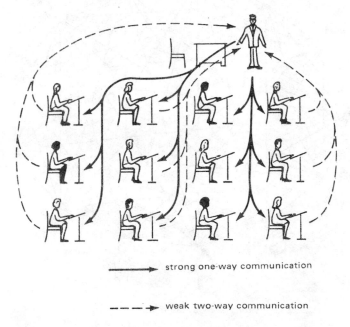

————————▶ strong one-way communication

— — — ▶ weak two-way communication

Figure 5a.  Social System: Teacher Domination

subject matter. All, or almost all, communication flows through him, and he makes most decisions as to PROCESS, including what will be done, where it will be done, how it will be done, and by whom it will be done.

The students, for the most part, act in response to his cues. From this response—even when negative—they develop ATTI-TUDES and reinforce the norms of position behavior that are inherent in the STRUCTURE. The teacher plans—the students obey without question except for clarification; the teacher lectures—students take notes; the teacher tests—the students take exams; the teacher evaluates—the students wait to find out whether or not they learned anything.

Changing the STRUCTURE, as in Figure 5b, changes PRO-CESS (though it will take many students some time to get used

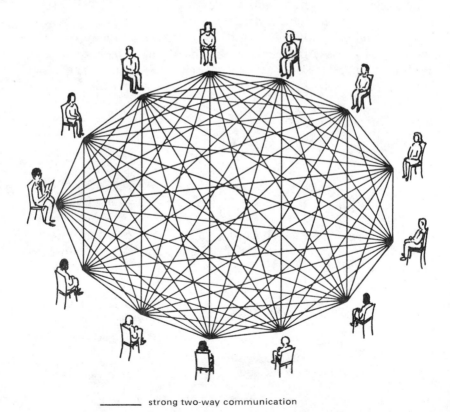

_____ strong two-way communication

**Figure 5b.** Social System: Teacher as Special Group Member

to the change) and eventually changes ATTITUDES. In this changed STRUCTURE, the students have more responsibility. They talk to each other as well as to the teacher, all communication does not have to flow through the teacher, and there is more student participation expected in terms of planning, executing, and evaluating.

In the cohesive learning group, the teacher by no means relinquishes control or ultimate responsibility.[4] Rather, he shares these with the students as junior partners or apprentices and teaches them how to respond in this more democratic situation. His behavior changes from dictator to that of most valuable of many group resources.

### The Framework

A theory of interaction begins with the actors and the pattern within which they interact. For our purposes we shall call these *Participant Backgrounds* and *Aggregate Structure.* These givens comprise the INITIAL SITUATION.

From this situation (the class and its teacher on the first meeting day) *Interaction* begins, and both teacher and students bring *Norm Inputs* into play. Obvious norms (acceptable ways of behaving) would include quieting down when the opening bell rings, raising hands to be called on, refraining from speech while the teacher is talking, sitting one behind the other and facing toward the front of the room, and asking permission before leaving seats or room. Other norms might include teacher asking questions and students answering, teacher as assignment giver and students as assignment doers, teacher as discipline giver and students as discipline receivers, girls as subgroup on one side of room and boys as subgroup on the other.

*Norm Inputs* (efforts to change or to reinforce existing

---

[4] For an exploration of the concept of status-leader behavior in the group setting see Alfred H. Gorman, *The Leader in the Group* (New York: Bureau of Publications, Teachers College, Columbia University, 1963). Probably one of the greatest blocks to democratic teaching is the teacher's fear that he will lose control and respect. This fear is a real one and cannot be dismissed lightly, but it should not block action. In the creation of a cohesive learning group, the teacher changes his role from dominance to guidance; *he does not merely abandon his class to their own devices.*

norms) evoke *Reactions* and *Try-Out Behaviors.* Students (out of their *Participant Backgrounds* and experience of the *Aggregate Structure*) may react to the teacher as strict, easy, fair, unfair, demanding, non-demanding, pleasant, nasty. The teacher (out of his personal background and his understanding of the structure demanded by his superiors) reacts to the class as easy, difficult, intelligent, stupid, noisy, well-behaved, fresh, obedient. Questions behind *Try-Out Behaviors* might include, on the student's part: "What can I get away with?" "How can I impress the teacher and get a good grade?" On the teacher's part:

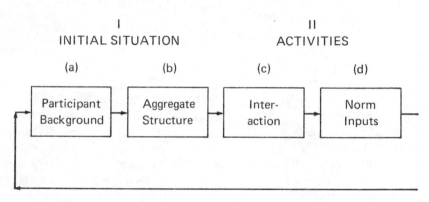

| I<br>INITIAL SITUATION | | II<br>ACTIVITIES | |
| :---: | :---: | :---: | :---: |
| (a) | (b) | (c) | (d) |
| Participant<br>Background | Aggregate<br>Structure | Inter-<br>action | Norm<br>Inputs |

Cycling Process:  Behavior change affects the initial situation which in turn affects further activities, and feedback on further activities points the way to further behavior change.

| Participant<br>Background | Aggregate<br>Structure | Inter-<br>action | Norm<br>Inputs |
| :--- | :--- | :--- | :--- |
| What the teacher and students bring with them to their first meeting in terms of knowledge, understanding, skills, attitudes, appreciations, self-concepts, intelligence, ways of behaving, expectations, social and academic needs. | Initially expected and accepted norms of behavior for teachers and students. Accepted procedures such as teacher planning, use of texts, oral class recitation, seating arrangements, general student immobility for class period. | Verbal (and non-verbal by means of facial expression and body attitudes) communication between teacher and students and among students. | Efforts by both students and teacher either to reinforce or change the aggregate structure of (b). Efforts center on control and direction of activities. |

**Figure 6.** A Theoretical Framework for Classroom Interaction

"How permissive can I be?" "How can I maintain discipline?" "How can I get them to participate?"

Through *Interaction* (blocked and/or facilitated), *Norm Inputs, Reactions,* and *Try-Out Behaviors,* ways of behaving in this particular class are worked through, and *Norm Acceptance—* or at least temporary *Norm Acceptance—*occurs. It may turn out to be a noisy, poorly behaved class; a quiet, threatened aggregate; a friendly, relaxed group; or some combination of these and other characteristics. Its resultant—or end step—is *Behavior Change.* Figure 6 shows these eight increments in dia-

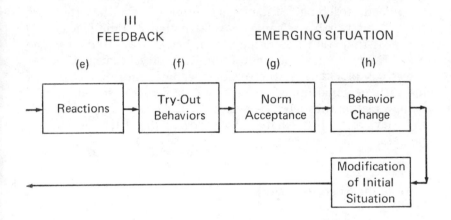

| III FEEDBACK | | IV EMERGING SITUATION | |
|---|---|---|---|
| (e) | (f) | (g) | (h) |
| Reactions | Try-Out Behaviors | Norm Acceptance | Behavior Change |

Modification of Initial Situation

|  Reactions | Try-Out Behaviors | Norm Acceptance | Behavior Change |
|---|---|---|---|
| Teacher and student feelings about the effectiveness and satisfaction of the interaction process in the class. | Efforts growing out of needs and feelings to get to know each other better, to test limits of control, to reinforce agreeable norm inputs, and to change those which are disagreeable. | Establishment of general norms and climate of this particular class. Support by both teacher and students of certain ways of behaving. | Change or reinforcement of the Initial Situation. Change—or resistance to change —occurs both on the cognitive (intellectual) and on the affective (emotional-social) levels. |

gramatic form. Progress—or lack of progress—proceeds from left to right (from INITIAL to EMERGING SITUATION). The INITIAL SITUATION is modified (changed or reinforced) and the process is repeated with a new INITIAL SITUATION proceeding toward a new EMERGING SITUATION. The quality of each EMERGING SITUATION throughout the year of schooling depends upon the positive and/or negative inputs of the teacher and the students as they interact in the classroom setting.

Not all behavior change, of course, is what the teacher planned for, nor is the teacher always clearly aware of what he is, indeed, teaching. Students sometimes learn that they are stupid and worthless, some may learn that reading is a boring waste of time, and others may learn better ways to disrupt the class. Cognitive learning may be in difficulty because affective growth is blocked. As the teacher becomes more conscious of his own personal impact on students and of the social climate being created through interaction in his classroom, he will be more aware of just what is occurring in the teaching-learning process.

## Putting the Theory to Work

To illustrate the components of the framework in terms of teacher perception, imagine yourself as a teacher waiting for your students to arrive for the first class session. You are determined to be friendly, but firm. You will be pleasant and responsive, but you will be in control at all times and discipline problems will be met promptly and decisively.

### Teacher-Centered Teaching

(a)   Based on your success in college and the good feedback you have had on the job for the last few years, you view yourself as a competent teacher. You enjoy teaching, expect satisfaction and no great problems with this class which is a high ability group. Having checked guidance records, you feel that at least two students are potential behavior problems. You will see that they sit apart from each other.

(b)   Your expectations are that the students will be orderly and obedient, that they will sit in rows, one behind the other, and that they will settle down quickly and get to work. You will not let them choose seats, but will seat them alphabetically to break up possible cliques in addition to the two potential behavior problems. You will make a little speech telling them what you expect and outlining the first unit of work. Then you will hand out the books and go through them. Finally, you will give the first homework assignment along with the form you wish them to use in doing it. The final bell is *your* signal. They must wait for *your* dismissal.

(c)   The class files in. You study them and they seem to be studying you. You do your alphabetical seating, and they groan—but not too loudly. One student suggests that they sit where *they* want to, and you say that this is *your* way of seating. Perhaps, in the future, there can be some changes. As you outline the first unit, hands go up for a number of questions. You shut off questions until the end of the presentation so that time will not run out. At the final bell, they jump from their seats, and you have to call them back for a little lecture. They look at each other and smile, but they do not object out loud.

(d)   During the next few sessions, you follow up the norms of (1) waiting until you are finished talking before asking questions, and (2) remaining seated at the final bell until *you* give the word. You give them a few of your rules: (1) no gum chewing; (2) raising hands to be recognized; (3) no talking to other students except at certain times; and (4) doing homework only on school paper folded once down the middle. You then further outline their responsibilities for the unit and give out book report forms. One of the potential behavior problems fails to pay close attention, and he talks incessantly to his neighbors. After warning him twice, you react to his tickling the boy in front of him by sending him to the office from which he returns seemingly disciplined. During the first week, the class, which was just a bit noisy at first, begins to be more quiet and orderly.

(e)   As the first couple of weeks go by, you begin to get a feel for and a reaction to the class. They are a little hard to deal with because they think they know it all, claim that some of your approaches are boring, and constantly try to put you on the spot with complicated questions.

(f)    You are determined to be boss here. These youngsters are not going to run the class. Perhaps, if you cut some of the leaders down with sarcasm when they ask complicated questions, this business of putting you on the spot will stop. Probably, some difficult assignments will help put them in their place. You will act stern without smiling until you gain more control. Then, you will be able to ease up and be more yourself.

(g)    As the first month draws to a close, you feel satisfied that you are now in control of the class. They hand in their work on time and in the proper form, and they no longer ask questions to put you on the spot. Only three things bother you, and you will have to work on them. They are: (1) once when you stepped out of the room briefly you returned to a disorderly situation where the students were throwing papers at each other; (2) whenever you try to work individually with one student, the noise level increases so that you have to stop; and (3) now that you have eased up and expect student participation, no one volunteers. Perhaps they are not so bright after all.

(h)    The students have learned how you want them to behave in your class, and you have learned that your approach works but that there are some undesirable side effects. You feel in control but not at ease. Whenever you become permissive they seem to take advantage. Perhaps you should have tried to get the leaders on your side rather than squelching them. This will be your next attempt.

By the time you and the class have reached (h) a climate has been set, and behaviors of the INITIAL SITUATION have been modified or reinforced. Efforts at norm setting have gone through the initial reaction and the try-out stage, and the class has reached some kind of plateau either through a total group consensus or through a teacher-student armed truce.

At this point, the cycle returns us to (a) which is Participant Background *Second Stage* and to (b) which is now *Aggregate-Group* Structure. The Participant Background (always including the teacher as a participant) has changed, and it has changed in such a way that a group is beginning to form out of the initial aggregate. How far the aggregate has moved toward group status will depend on the ratio between blocking and facilitating behaviors on the part of the participants. In the example above, for instance, the teacher keeps his feelings to himself and prevents students from expressing theirs either to him or to each other. This blocking of expressed feelings tends to maintain the aggregate (formal interaction with everyone on guard) and deny opportunities for group formation (informal as well as formal interaction with participants free to express negative and positive feelings and motivated to resolve problems through consensus rather than carry on an undeclared power struggle).

It is the intent of the author to suggest ways in which communication can be improved. The class climate of the example above cannot be changed merely by having the teacher ease up and smile a lot. There is no assurance that a more permissive teacher would not be overrun and taken advantage of by this class. Looseness and lack of teacher direction is not a good alternative to tightness and overdirection. What is needed is the development of a climate in which participants can disagree *and* go on to *resolve* problems of control, motivation, behavior, and structure. In order to promote this kind of climate (movement toward becoming a group), the participants need to engage in two-way communication which will introduce a norm of open discussion of what is going on and how everyone feels about it. The notion of *making* this a norm rests on the assumption that it will not *just happen.* Both teacher and students are accustomed to a norm of one-way communication from the teacher, little or no expression of feeling, and teacher use of power rather than group consensus in decision making. Thus, the "democratic" teacher who walks into a classroom and declares that it will be run in a democratic fashion should not be surprised when the students do not know how to deal with freedom. They have to be taught to deal with democratic freedoms and obligations just as they have to be taught reading or mathematics. Similarly, an aggregate does not just become a group by being together through time. Some teaching and learning must occur first. Notice the results of teaching (norm inputs) and learning (norm development) in the example above. If the outcome here is an autocratic climate, it has not happened by accident—it was carefully taught and learned. The sad thing is that this teacher is probably unaware of the damage he is doing in his quest for control and order. He could certainly benefit by being less uptight and more permissive. The reader should note at this point, however, that permissiveness alone is not the answer. Indeed, mere permissiveness may be worse than autocratic control. What, then, is a better approach?

The following example outlines an attempt to establish a climate which is more group than aggregate. One central point should be kept in mind: A group (as opposed to an aggregate) is a good place to be and a good place to learn, *but it is not problem free.* No collection of people can expect to operate together through time without developing problems. A group has problems just as an aggregate does—*the difference lies in the agreed-upon mechanisms for solving the problems.* In the aggregate, problems are met with manipulation or raw use of teacher power. They are not resolved by the group openly, but rather denied or bulldozed out of the way. In the group, problems are explored, alternative answers suggested by all, and solutions arrived at by consensus. The following is one way to proceed: Here you are again imagining yourself as a teacher waiting for your students to arrive for the first class session. You are determined to help this aggregate of students and teacher mature as a group. You have strong feelings concerning control and discipline, but you realize that students also have feelings. You believe that class activities are best directed and controlled by *both* teacher *and* students.

## Group-Centered Teaching

(a)   Based on successes and failure both in college and on the teaching job, you have a positive image of yourself. You are not the best teacher in the world, but you are pretty good, and you have confidence, based on good experience, in letting students know how you feel even when the feeling is unsureness or insecurity. You know that the incoming students are alike in IQ but that they are bound to be very different human beings with natural feelings both good and bad about themselves and about the schooling process.

(b)   Your expectations are that these students are familiar with norms that seat them one behind the other, do not allow them to talk to one another, and set the teacher up as dominator. You value a norm which allows more student-to-student interaction and which sees the teacher as a special member of the group. You feel that you have to begin with some familiar structure, but that you should begin to challenge it early.

(c) The class files in. You study them, and they seem to be studying you. You tell them your name plus a sentence or two concerning how you feel about coming back to school. Then, you ask them if they would each like to say their names and a brief feeling about being here. Then, you ask them to form groups of four by choosing classmates they do not know so well. The task of the fours is to get to know each other and talk about expectations of what they will do in this class. Each quartet is to make a written list. While groups meet, you spend a brief time with each. Each written list is made on a ditto master so that they can be run off for all members of the class.

(d) At the second session—or later in the day for a self-contained classroom—you say that you have many ideas of how the class should be run and what it should study just as they have and that decisions should be made by all members of the class including yourself. You suggest that seating is optional—that the seats and desks can stay as they are or be changed into a big U or O shape so that everyone can see everyone else. You then ask them how they wish to proceed with the written expectations and the seating and anything else that seems important to them. Then you stop talking and let them wrestle with this freedom. When they ask you questions, you reflect them back to the students and avoid taking the dominant role. (See nondirective discussion leadership, pp. 131-139.)

(e) As the first couple of weeks go by, you begin to get a feel for and a reaction to the class. As feelings occur to you, you share them with the class. If you feel that they are having a hard time being active rather than passive learners, you say it and ask how they are feeling. If you feel that some student's behavior is a problem to you, you say this and ask help in solving the problem. You use written unsigned reaction sheets or ask them to write you short letters in order to find out how they feel about you and the class and what, if anything, they would like changed. You respond to these reactions by taking action or by class discussion of the items.

(f) You respond readily to suggestions and try out various ways of behaving as a teacher, getting written and verbal feedback as you proceed. You avoid labeling such as: "You are misbehaving," and try, instead, to say things like: "Your talking is making me feel that what I am saying is not worth much. What can we do about it?" Your attempt is to get students to follow your model of giving even negative feelings openly but also being responsible for offering alternatives to whatever is not liked. Your intent is that they learn to deal with feelings productively without labeling people or putting them down. "What we're doing stinks" is honest feedback, but it is both hurtful and unclear. There are better ways of stating a feeling such as: "I like the idea of what we're doing, but I'm frustrated because the instructions are still not clear to me."

(g) As the first month draws to a close, you feel good about what is going on. The students are working through their problems in being self-directing, and communication is getting slowly more open *and* more productive. The students are beginning to trust you because you have not ever pulled back and started to issue orders even when they have said some negative things about your teaching. Some students still show a need to be told what to do, and there are three students who disrupt what others are trying to do. There is, however, a growing norm of working together and sharing feelings. When a new student came into the class in the third week and used the unaccustomed freedom to clown, some of your students took him aside in a nice way and told him that, "We just don't act that way in this class." The whole class has identified an area they want to study and has asked you to lecture on it for three days as an introduction. You have agreed as long as they will discuss it afterwards and tell you how you might have done it better. Instead of being apprehensive of such evaluation, as you thought you might be when you began such an approach, you look forward to it with eagerness.

(h)   The students have learned how you want them to behave, *and you have learned how they want to behave.* The approach being used is not yours alone but a composite of your ideas and those of the students. It is still largely your show, but more and more students are learning how to get into the act effectively. Some would still like more teacher direction, and you are wondering what to do about that. You are learning how to be democratic without being overly permissive and without going too fast for the students who are so used to being told what to do all the time.

This teacher approach also sets a climate by the time the class and teacher have reached point (h). Participant Background has changed, and the Aggregate-Group Structure is very far along the way toward group status. Problems have by no means disappeared, but there is widespread support for the open expression of feelings, and the class has had some good experiences in resolving problems. *Cognitive* knowledge, as measured by a variety of measurement devices prepared by students as well as teacher, is very good. It could be better, but motivation is high and students are doing a good job of learning how to learn. *Affective* knowledge, also measured by teacher and students, is growing and becoming increasingly effective in classroom use.

It is important to note at this point that the interactions referred to in the framework are *not* activities carried out *in addition to* ordinary teaching and learning procedures. They *are* these ordinary procedures to which the elements of analysis, evaluation, and retesting have been added. In the traditional class, these elements are already applied to the cognitive aspects of learning. The theory above suggests that this is not enough to foster a good learning situation. Noting that cognitive aspects are interwoven with affective, or emotional, aspects, it calls for a better balance in dealing with these co-factors than has existed historically in the school.

Since even the most traditional classroom includes some interaction and group growth, the framework is useful in any schooling situation. To the usual class setting, it introduces a focus on three vital elements: (1) the initial and emerging attitudinal and feeling tone of the learning group; (2) the notion of affect feedback; and (3) the use of situation change analysis to affect ongoing activities.

Such a set of procedures can serve to highlight for both teacher and students what is excellent, what is merely good, and what is poor in any teaching approach. In addition, it provides ways of creatively dealing with interaction problems as they are identified.

## Aims of Improved Classroom Interaction[5]

Before leaving the theory and proceeding to methodology, it would seem helpful to specify some of the aims that prompt professional teachers to take the time to improve interaction in the classroom. What is sought . . .

. . . in the area of teaching and learning is:

| a movement from: | toward: |
| --- | --- |
| teacher domination | teacher as special member of group |
| teacher as sole leader | group-centered shared leadership |
| extrinsic control in hands of teacher | intrinsic control in hands of individuals (including teacher) |
| active membership of teacher plus two or three verbal students | active membership of total group |
| stress on subject with exclusion of personal social needs | stress on both cognitive and affective elements |
| almost total dependence on teacher as planner, initiator, and evaluator | student self-direction and independence |

[5] For a formulation of objectives drawn from a similar framework of learning see Association for Supervision and Curriculum Development, *Perceiving, Behaving, Becoming*, Yearbook (Washington, D.C.: The Association, 1962), "Signs of Creative Teaching," p. 237.

formal recitation by small percentage of students

spontaneous participation by all

selective inattention by students

careful listening with feedback checks

an aggregate of noncohesive individuals

a cohesive group of interacting individuals

student learning with the intent of test passing and grade setting

student learning to satisfy personal needs to know and to grow

. . . in the area of emotional growth is:

| a movement from: | toward: |
| --- | --- |
| guarded, hidden feelings | a norm of openness and spontaneous expression of feelings |
| unchecked assumptions | positive feelings that assumptions should be checked |
| neutral feelings toward the meaningfulness of the learning experience | positive feelings that the experience has personal meanings and values |
| neutral feelings toward the class group | positive, warm response toward others ("my group" feeling) |
| vague student anxiety: "Who am I in this group?" | personal security: "I am I, accepted and valued" |
| preoccupation with self and with projection of "good" self-image | sensitivity to verbally and nonverbally expressed needs of others |
| student fear of speaking in a group situation | confidence in expressing feelings, knowledge, and direction |
| view of teacher as nonhuman object | view of teacher as human being with feelings similar to those of students |

Having dealt with the theory and with some of the aims connected with it, we can now proceed to practice. In the following chapters, the intent is to present detailed plans for developing classroom interaction, extending and deepening the process, evaluating activities, and feeding the evaluation back into the circular process inherent in the framework. And finally, since any text is only a beginning for the imaginative teacher, guidelines are suggested for the student who wishes to create approaches and exercises specifically suited to his personal needs.

# chapter 3

# Classroom Interaction Processes

Any approach to working with groups should begin with a concept of what groups are all about, move on to formulate general objectives concerning ultimate goals, and finally state specific objectives underlying the particular approach being applied. These beginning concerns are what this chapter is about.

### Group Variables

Group has been partially defined in Chapter 1 as a collection of people who interact with each other, are fairly free to express *feelings* as well as *thoughts*, act without fear of judgmental reactions by others, and cut through ritualized games that people generally learn to play with each other. As Figure 6 suggests, participants sitting down together for a first session come with a variety of experiences and attitudes. They do not become a group by merely coming together. Proximity and time are needed but, even with these, the aggregate may not reach group status. Specific normative inputs (acceptable procedures and ways of behaving) are needed, and, in the classroom, this task usually falls to the teacher as one of the most knowledgeable of the aggregate leaders at the outset.

    Both internal and external variables affect the growth of an aggregate toward grouphood. External group variables would include the general cultural values, the varied and conflicting values of the immediate community, general expectations of schooling, and the specific expectations of a specific school. While these variables are most significant in their influence on the maturing aggregate, they are outside the scope of the present material which has its focus on the group-as-a-group. We shall, therefore, address ourselves only to internal group variables.

Any classroom aggregate faces a similar set of problems as they begin their interactions. They must, out of their individual backgrounds and perceptions plus their mutual activity, create a process for communicating in addition to norms for determining which individual behaviors they will accept and which they will ignore or reject. In doing this, they may or may not employ skill, and they may or may not increase the beginning level of skill of the participants. The sum total of these efforts, the reactions of participants to the efforts, and the trying out of behaviors creates the group-feeling tone, or climate. Internal group variables include:

1. Membership Characteristics
2. Communications Network
3. Accepted Ways of Behaving
4. Communication Skills
5. Climate

## Membership Characteristics

One of the most frequently told school anecdotes concerns the teacher who has a great success in one of his classes—a smooth satisfying experience in which everything goes well, everyone participates, and there is a general feeling of good will and accomplishment. Glowing with the realization that teaching can be a glorious experience, the teacher walks into a second class, behaves in precisely the same way, and the whole operation falls flat.

This situation seems to occur often enough to deserve serious attention. Looking past the sea of faces turned in various states of attention toward the teacher, an observer can see a host of differing personalities, each formed by heredity and personal reactions to environment past and present. Given these types of individual differences plus a teacher response solely in terms of subject-matter presentation and corrective disciplinary control, it is not strange that free, open communication is blocked in so many classrooms. Yet openness and personal meaning does occur occasionally, as in the instance of the anecdote. Where the teacher makes his error is in supposing that his actions alone caused the positive situation. If this were true, then he would have no trouble in transferring the wonderful moment to any or all of his other classes. But members vary from group to group, and this quality is a vital ingredient of the learning situation.

Involved closely with differing personalities of members are differing attitudes and expectations toward both self and situation. Does the teacher really know these aspects of his students? Do his students know each other in these terms? How can such knowing affect behavior? In what direction? What would be the result of ignoring student expectations? Can initial expectations be changed? These are pressing questions for the teacher.

Beyond personalities, attitudes, and expectations, but closely connected with them, is the perception of group status. Each member of any group seeks clarification of his individual place in the total scheme. He asks: Who am I in this group? What do people expect of me? What power, if any, do I have? How free can I be to express my real feelings? Do other members respect me? Who will support me? Who will really understand? To whom can I turn? These are important questions to each student, and when they are not clearly defined they often lead to withdrawal, deviant behavior, clique formation, and/or resistance to teacher direction.

To summarize, membership is a variable based upon what each individual brings with him to a group and what happens to him and to others as a result of his being there.

## Communications Network

Studies by Hughes[1] and others have found that typical American teacher behavior is *telling*, and that typical American stu-

[1] Marie Hughes et al., *Development of the Means for Assessment of the Quality of Teaching in Elementary Schools* (Salt Lake City: University of

dent behavior is *listening*. This notion of teaching as telling is reinforced by the egg-crate school, the rows of student desks, the larger teacher desk, and the teacher's position at the front of the room. Given this traditional and rarely questioned setting, it should not come as a surprise that American classrooms resemble a "story hour" rather than a working group.

Place a teacher at the head of rows of seated, listening students, and the communication pattern resembles Figure 5a, page 37. Seat everyone in a circle or in a series of circles and the network changes. As in the instance of group climate, however, the mere physical change of seats does not significantly alter the way communication takes place in a classroom. What is important is what group members *do* when the physical arrangement is changed. Many teachers skim through a book on group processes, circle their students, and continue to lecture. Or students sit in a series of circles helplessly wasting time until the teacher comes over and tells them what to do. The teacher (who traditionally has done most of the communicating) must accept the responsibility for teaching students how to communicate in various settings if he is to change the network or flow of messages in his classroom.

Aspects of the prevailing network in any group include ways in which people participate and the freedom people feel in contributing ideas. These aspects also affect the kind of participation. Do students merely answer teacher questions? Do they speak freely to each other? Do they elaborate, clarify, summarize, and otherwise help the verbal interaction, or are these functions mostly left to the teacher? Does the teacher do most of the talking? Are there efforts to support and encourage members to participate? Is the prevailing network ever analyzed or questioned? Is anything done to improve conditions?

To summarize, the communication network is instrumental in determining the type and amount of participation and interaction in a classroom. It raises the question of who talks to whom, with what intent, and with what result.

Utah, 1959). See also Arno A. Bellack et al., *The Language of the Classroom: Meanings Communicated in High School Teaching*, U.S. Department of Health, Education and Welfare, Office of Education, Cooperative Research Project no. 1497 (New York: Institute of Psychological Research, Columbia University, 1963).

## Accepted Ways of Behaving

Norms of behavior are too frequently spelled out by the teacher through a list of do's and don'ts. Such class norms are usually developed in terms of the teacher's notion of acceptable behavior. Nevertheless, in cooperation with the teacher, or sometimes in defiance of him, students influence greatly the norms of any classroom. The students may act as individuals or cliques and produce a norm of noncooperation, or they may act together and against the teacher. Their battle cry may be, "We got Mr. Williams to explode in fifteen minutes yesterday. Let's see if we can break our own record today."

Writers such as Coleman[2] have described the peer culture in the schools, and it seems a force to be reckoned with, yet teachers untrained in this area tend to avoid the problem by pretending that nothing is really going on in the class but the teaching of mathematics or whatever. Peer norms certainly seem to affect individual dress and attitudes, and, in more subtle ways, they affect classroom behavior. It may be the unspoken notion in Mr. Brown's class that a student who participates is apple polishing, and apple polishing is forbidden. Thus, those students who wish to ask questions, give information, or make comments are inhibited unless they feel that they can stand alone against the sanctions employed by their fellow students.

While the teacher, as appointed leader, acts to impose certain norms, emerging leadership on the part of one or more students also can exert effective pressure. The present writer observed an instance of this while visiting a student teacher who had been assigned a "problem" class. One tall student who sat in the front seat nearest the door apparently did a good deal of the class management with nonverbal signs. He had aligned himself, for the day at least, on the side of the student teacher and was determined that the class would behave itself. As the lesson went on, various individuals and cliques began irrelevant behavior which could have grown into incidents calling for disciplinary action. The student leader knew his group, how-

[2] James S. Coleman, *The Adolescent Society: The Social Life of the Teenager and Its Impact on Education* (New York: Free Press, 1961). A look at the values of students, which often conflict and rarely connect with the values of their teachers. Interesting insight into a peer culture.

ever, and a glance or frown or slight hand gesture cut off each potential explosion. At the end of the class, the student teacher glowed. "Problem class, bah," she said. "All they need is a businesslike approach and an interesting lesson."

This anecdote does not depreciate in any way the need for a teacher's being interesting and businesslike, but it does highlight the norm-developing potential of groups and the influence of emerging leadership. In the spate of materials and "crash programs" that have focused on the "gifted child" following the Russian orbiting of Sputnik I, the idea of the "gifted student leader" who might benefit by specific instruction and guided experiences has been largely unexplored. Whether or not such specific programs get off the ground in the near future, it would seem that present teachers could benefit by understanding and making use of peer leadership and peer pressures rather than ignoring them or opposing them.

To summarize, generalized knowledge of appropriate ways of behaving by both teacher and students is essential as an aggregate extends itself through time. While the most overt expression of norms, at least in the early stages, comes traditionally from the teacher, much influence is exercised by the other group members and the emerging student leaders. Where communication is unclear, generalized group norms are difficult to develop and cliques may form or the class may unite against the teacher. It would seem reasonable to assume that the effectiveness of a group norm increases in proportion to the number of people involved in producing it. If the teacher insists on setting norms all by himself (e.g., no gum chewing in my class), he will still have to either sell the idea to the students or use his authority to enforce it. If the teacher *and* the students set the norm, *all* group members will support it.

## Communication Skills

The sender's intent, his assumptions, his message, and its reception are dealt with in Chapter 2. Awareness of the difficulties involved in effective communication is an important first step, but the development of verbal skills demands the deepening of awareness plus practice. Such skills include listening, clarifying, testing consensus, problem diagnosis, and the general refinement of ability to convey one's ideas to others in the way one intends them to be received.[3]

In the formation of a group out of the beginning aggregate member skill is a vital consideration. Too often, teachers attempt a "democratic approach" without thinking of or accepting the responsibility for helping students to gain the verbal interpersonal skills necessary to operate a classroom democracy. It is not enough for the teacher to announce that, *"This is going to be a class where we plan together and work together." Having been manipulated in the past, they may not easily trust teachers. But even when students accept such a teacher statement at face value, they may feel inadequate to respond to such a proposal.* In order really to plan and work with the teacher they will have to have or develop skills in discussion participation; ways of distributing responsibilities for work to be done; and ways of problem solving, decision making, and evaluating what they have done. Before taking away the comfortable crutch of teacher domination, the professional teacher (providing that he really desires to share the leadership and responsibility in a democratic manner) will begin, with his students, to build communication skills so that the group may move forward in terms of efficiency and satisfaction.

To summarize, communication skills involve verbal and nonverbal interactions that get across individual messages in the way the senders intend them and that encourage the participation of the total membership in the work of the group.


## Climate

Among the many criticisms of administrators (and these abound joyously in the folklore of schooling) is the description of the principal who prowls the halls expecting all classes to be "quiet and orderly" and woe to the careless teacher who is found sitting on his desk. Many present educators can remember the time when children were compelled to clasp their hands before them on their desks, and each chair was secured firmly to the floor to prevent any disruptive student movement which might

[3] With reference to the conveying of one's ideas, see the discussion on pp. 23-24 of this book.

break the semi-religious aura of "good behavior" and "serious teaching."

To such restrictive atmospheres, the progressive educators of the 1920's brought a sharp reversal in terms of permissiveness and child-centeredness. Hands were unclasped, and even gross body movements were allowed while students were asked what *they* wanted to learn. In some cases, this abrupt removal of rigid structure from above resulted in warm, happy atmospheres where people sought learning without being driven to it; in other situations, unhappy chaos resulted. The restrictive, the warm, the happy, the chaotic climates are seen in clear outlines in Lewin's study of the results of authoritarian, democratic, and laissez-faire leadership.[4]

Of course, the attitudes of the members (always including the teacher as member extraordinary) have a great deal to do with the type of climate developed by a classroom group. Endless arguments concerning over-traditional versus soupy progressive teacher approaches do not really end by clarifying anything. More to the point is the realization that members develop climates similar to those with which they have become familiar. The sensitive teacher, schooled in group processes, will help the group to assess the prevailing climate, leaving the way open for change if it seems desirable to most members. On the other hand, such assessment combined with a notion of freedom of decision arouses a fear reaction in some teachers. Such fears usually act to cut communication and substitute a "Let's pretend that everything's fine" game. Concern over control of students sometimes results in the "Don't smile until Christmas to show 'em who's boss" syndrome. A similar but more subtle response to the fear that students will when given free choice always choose aimless play over rigorous learning leads to the "No nonsense—we have to cover the ground" approach. (It should be noted that not all students are ready for democratic procedures in the classroom. Many actively fear and resist personal freedom and responsibility, thus making the work of the progressive teacher a challenge indeed.)

In any case, a climate is developed as people spend time

---

[4] Ronald Lippitt and Ralph K. White, "The Social Climate of Children's Groups," in Roger Barker, Jacob Kounin, and Herbert Wright, *Child Development and Behavior* (New York: McGraw-Hill Book Co., 1943).

together and break through the initial formal, "ice-breaking" period. More often than not, freedom of expression does not develop in the classroom so that the atmosphere develops out of unchecked assumptions and unstated or unclearly stated desires and expectations. It is true that time helps an aggregate become more of a group. No aggregate becomes a group during its first few sessions regardless of the techniques employed. But more than time is needed. No aggregate becomes a group *merely* because of the passage of time.

If a highly formal classroom atmosphere persists, it can lead to tenseness and produce indifference, suspicion, clique formation, inhibition of cognitive as well as emotional responses, and finally result in frustration for all concerned.

The development of an informal climate on the other hand can lead to group loyalty, a feeling of mutual trust, freedom of expression on both cognitive and emotional levels, total group cohesion, and finally satisfaction by all concerned. (Note that, at this point, the reader should automatically include the teacher in the word *all.*)

Proof that each group is a product of its particular members lies in the fact that formal and informal atmospheres do not automatically produce the results suggested in the preceding paragraphs. People can be productive in formal settings and quite uncomfortable in relaxed climates. The professional teacher avoids the semantic trap of playing games with words like *formal* and *informal* and works with his aggregate to produce a climate that acts optimally to satisfy both social and cognitive needs (always including his own).

To summarize, climate is a variable produced by the expectations of members modified by their perceptions of the present situation and their degree of interaction and communication.

*Internal Group Variables*

In outline form, the five aspects of group communication discussed above would be as follows:

1.  Membership Characteristics:
    Personalities
    Attitudes
    Expectations
    Perceptions of relative status

2. Communication Network:
   Who talks to whom?
   Who leads?
   Who follows?
   Is leadership shared?
   Who is quiet or withdrawn?
   Is everyone involved?
   Is there concern to involve all members?
   Who expresses this concern—teacher or members or both?
   Is the major pattern:
   (a)  Teacher ⎯⎯⎯⎯⎯→ Students?
   (b)  Teacher ←⎯⎯⎯⎯→ Students?

   (c)  Teacher ⎯⎯⎯ Student
        Student ⎯⎯⎯ Student

3. Accepted Ways of Behaving:
   Individual expectations
   Individual needs
   Norm development
        by teacher
        by students
        by teacher and students

4. Communication Skills:
   Diagnosing problems which block the group
   Listening
   Involving nonparticipators
   Clarifying and elaborating ideas
   Giving recognition and support
   Summarizing
   Keeping discussion on track
   Consensus testing
   Harmonizing group issues
These skills are used in specific group tasks such as:
   Planning
   Agenda setting
   Distribution of responsibilities
   Problem solving
   Decision making
   Meeting members' personal social needs
   Evaluating periodically and as a culminating activity

5. Climate:
   Perceptions by group members on a continuum between feelings of:
   Formality ⎯⎯⎯⎯⎯ and—Informality

| | |
|---|---|
| Tenseness ——————— | and—Relaxation |
| Indifference ——————— | and—Loyalty |
| Suspicion ——————————————— | and—Trust |
| Inhibition ——————————————— | and—Freedom of Expression |
| Isolation and clique formation——— | and—Total Group Cohesion |
| Frustration ——————————————— | and—Satisfaction |

These five sets of variables are interlocking and at times overlapping. They occur in every classroom setting, though group members rarely seem to understand them clearly or seek to make them explicit. Once they are identified and discussed by the group, however, there is a sharp increase in member feelings of reality as opposed to game-playing-until-the-bell-rings. When an aggregate is able to bring perceptions out into the open so that they can be dealt with, it is on its way to becoming a group. The first step in the analysis and understanding of the group situation is up to the teacher (appointed leader), and he himself needs understanding and the tools of analysis before he can take that first step.

The reader as teacher (appointed leader) is urged to do three things at this point: (1) reread the foregoing material on internal group variables and attempt to put the information in his own terms for the purpose of understanding, (2) add variables that occur to him (why not write in the book?), and (3) check the group-variables material against the framework on pp. 39-42. This framework begins with the background the members (always including the teacher) bring to the beginning sessions of the aggregate plus the physical and psychological structure that they also bring based on previous experiences. The theory of learning is contained in the cyclical process of initial situation, activities, feedback, emerging situation, further activities, further feedback, deepening of the emerging situation, further activities, further feedback, and so on, with the group situation becoming increasingly more clear, more productive, and more satisfying.

## Ultimate Goals

Though he may give lip service to a variety of idealistic statements of schooling purposes, a teacher's ultimate goals will flow from his own perceptions and attitudes. If he has received a good traditional education, he will more than likely enter the classroom not having worked out his teaching goals in any great depth. In general, he will want his students to learn the subject he will teach (this goal may mean a number of things according to how deeply he really knows his subject and how he personally defines learning), and he will want them to exhibit "good behavior" while they are doing it (and "good behavior" is certainly a relative term).

The interaction framework that underlies the methodology in this book views cognitive and emotional learning as interdependent. It calls for the analysis of the human factors of the learning group by the human beings involved in order to create a readiness and a methodology for dealing with the subject matter under consideration. Student (and teacher) learnings (yes, the teacher can learn in the classroom) begin in the area of group interaction and *then* move to the area of reading, spelling, mathematics, foreign language, home economics, or whatever. This approach differs from the traditional teaching-learning situation, which often treats the realities of human expectations, needs, and attitudes as if they did not exist. The theory does not, in any way, move away from a concentration on subject matter and ground to be covered. Rather, it seeks the help of all members (not merely the teacher) in making the classroom a more real situation wherein students, according to their maturity and ability to learn, will develop in themselves the motivation and the responsibility for their own learning activity. In such a setting, the teacher should be able to concentrate on teaching, and students should be able to concentrate on learning, which, after all, is what schooling is supposed to be all about.

Stemming from this theoretical approach, the following general objectives can be identified:

1. Improved interpersonal communication.
2. Sensitivity to the effects of member behavior in group settings.
3. Understanding of the dynamics of working groups.
4. Intellectual and emotional involvement in the learning process.

Learnings take place on both personal and interpersonal levels:

| Personal | Interpersonal |
|---|---|
| Understanding one's own feelings | Understanding feelings of others |
| Skill in communicating feelings | Skill in group task and maintenance behaviors |
| Self-direction | Ability to diagnose communication problems |
| Self-responsibility | |
| Intrinsic motivation | Full membership participation |

## Specific Objectives

A careful examination of the general objectives stated above reveals that they are written in terms of teaching; not in terms of teaching $x$ or teaching $y$ or teaching $z$, but in terms of just plain teaching. Put in another way, these objectives are concerned with the process of teaching rather than with its content. Such an emphasis does not deny the importance of content; rather, it seeks to focus on the process of teaching and learning the content, be it industrial arts, Latin, history, or another phase of the curriculum.

As background to a consideration of methodology in the following chapters, it is necessary: (1) to define process, (2) to specify the behaviors that make up process, and (3) to suggest a way to make these behaviors apparent so that they can be learned and improved.

## Process in Teaching and Learning

In any social situation, there are two levels on which communication takes place. The first and most familiar is the subject under discussion, or the *content level*; the second concerns the effects of member behavior on themselves and on the others, or the *process level*. When a teacher explains something on the chalkboard and encourages students to ask questions, and when a little girl does ask a question, and when the teacher brushes her aside by impatiently stating that this question has already been clearly answered, several communications have been made. On the content level, there has been explanation of the subject matter, a request for possible questions, a question, and an answer. On the process level, there has been a teacher denial of what he seemed to be asking for. Also, there has been an inhibiting of further student questions. Who wants to take the chance of being called stupid or of losing ground in the constant fight for high grades? Also, there has been a decrease in trust of the teacher; one had better take whatever he says in the future with a large grain of salt.

The terms *content level* and *process level* are used to pinpoint emphasis on fact or on feeling in human interaction. They could, as well, be called *topic level* (what is being discussed) and *reaction level* (what is being felt). Any communicative exchange between two people or among several includes both levels intermixed. In practical terms, the intellect and the emotions cannot be separated. People have knowledge of facts and concepts *and* they have feelings about themselves and others. For a variety of reasons, however, most people keep communication crowded over into the *content level*, ignoring, avoiding, or denying the bulk of the *process level* material present. This inefficient, lopsided way of communicating is taught and learned indirectly, and it is learned so well that few people question the system. Small children, commonly, are observed to express their positive and negative feelings as freely as they do their ideas. As they grow, however, they (we) lose this spontaneity and learn to operate almost exclusively on the *content level*. In this, they are "helped" by parents, clergymen, and teachers who provide what could be called *anti-affect education*. For those who wish to offer education which would better balance the two levels, a first step would be a more sophisticated awareness of what does indeed happen when people are communicating.

Imagine a first-year social studies teacher, for example, sitting in on her first department meeting. The members of the department are all older than she is and seem very confident. They are polite to her, but she still feels like an outsider. The department chairman is all business, not very warm, and a little scary. He has not said anything negative, but she does not feel a great deal of support from him. To make matters worse, the principal, a distant authority figure whom she has met only once, has decided to sit in on the meeting.

The department chairman dislikes and fears the principal who seems always to be against the chairman's efforts to change the curriculum offerings. Department members also come with a variety of feelings which they keep hidden. Mr. A. hates these meetings that seem to him never to get anywhere and that keep him from his golf game. Mrs. B. resents the chairman's constant efforts to meddle with the curriculum which she thinks is fine the way it is. She is happy to see the principal who, she thinks, will support her in any argument she has with the department chairman. Mr. C.'s primary interest is in impressing Miss D., and he loudly supports any ideas she throws out. Mr. E. would like to suggest a new course in pure sociology, but he will not take a chance of alienating the principal who might be against the idea.

With all these unresolved, undealt with feelings, this aggregate sits down to address itself to a possible revision of the social studies curriculum. On the content level, much is said about student needs and new ideas for curriculum offerings. On the process level, the principal and Mrs. B. gang up on the chairman, Mr. A. yawns a bit and pays little attention, Mr. C. agrees loudly with Miss C. even when she is irrelevant, and Mr. E. has little to contribute. The beginning teacher is a bit confused and dimly aware that there are undercurrents in the conversation. She finally takes advantage of a pause and throws in an idea, but people merely look at her and go on talking as if they had not heard. She sits silent for the remainder of the meeting, resenting the fact that no one responded to her idea and angry at herself for not speaking more and making a good impression.

While every department meeting may not contain this amount of blocked affect, it is plain that even a smaller amount can cut down sharply on the effectiveness of the communication, the problem solving, and the decision making that is necessary each time that people sit down to perform a joint task.

Aspects of the two levels in outline form would be:

## COMMUNICATION

| Content Level | Process Level |
| --- | --- |
| Facts | Feelings |
| Intellectual | Emotional |
| Topic Centered | Reaction Centered |

| Formal | Informal |
|--------|----------|
| Cognitive | Affective |
| Impersonal | Personal |
| Open Intent | Hidden Intent |

The notion of content and process levels of communication is important not because one is any better than the other but because both exist during any human communication and because instruction in dealing with the process level has been neglected. A massive schooling effort, focused on the content level, has been mounted by practically all modern societies, but process level—which is always present and which can easily block or distort content level messages—has been treated for the most part as if it did not exist. People are asked constantly to enter a classroom (or job) and communicate with others only on the content level. This command is impossible to obey in any real sense. None of us can park our feelings outside the door to be picked up later. What we *can* do is suppress direct and spontaneous *expression* of our feelings. Teachers—like other adults—have learned to suppress and to indirectly teach suppression to their students *because they have also come to accept such bottling up of feelings as normal.* But, then, illiteracy would also be "normal" if no one was ever taught to read and if those who tried to learn on their own were punished for their efforts. Any society concerned with the mental health of its individuals might do well to question a norm which denies process-level instruction to its young.

For many teachers, a discussion of student feelings (process level) to say nothing of their own seems a touchy subject, and the safest way to deal with feelings appears to be to pretend they do not exist—that the only thing going on in the classroom is the transmission of subject matter (content level). Despite the most elaborate pretense, however, other things *are* going on, and they come out in terms of inattention, withdrawal, refusal to do any more than the minimum requirements, and in overt "discipline problems." When these reactions become disruptive, the teacher is often forced to take action, but this action comes quite late, is usually punitive in nature, and may not be clearly seen in relation to its cause. A simple family illustration of this communications breakdown is seen in the father who, upon returning home at six in the evening, is asked to punish a young child who misbehaved at ten in the morning.

The teacher who screams at a misbehaving student, sends youngsters out of the room for deviant actions, changes seats, or keeps a whole class after school is often treating symptoms instead of causes. In point of fact, he may not even be treating the symptoms, but merely requesting that students keep them to themselves and cooperate in the game of "Let's pretend that none of us are ever affected emotionally by anything that goes on in this class." But many students just cannot play this game all the time, and so devices have been developed including banishment from the classroom, a trip to the principal or the dean of students or the guidance office, a session or sessions in a detention hall after school, or expulsion from school for a few days (after which the student returns to begin the process all over again). Little wonder that students drop out of school physically or psychologically.

No real magic has been developed to combat behavior problems—or processes that often make communication difficult—but our traditional wisdom does seem to support the notion that running away from or attempting to ignore difficult situations is of little help.

But recognizing them and dealing with them is not easy. Mere teacher determination to explore the process level of communication in a class will not assure instant success. What is needed in addition is the incorporation in the teacher's attitude structure of a belief that the exploration of the process level is important in a teaching-learning situation and a subsequent teacher mastery of techniques for such exploration. Presentation of techniques is the job of this book; teacher attitude change will come from study, further educative experiences, much trial, and the examination of errors.

## Content and Process Behaviors

Benne and Sheats and others[5] have identified *behaviors, functions,* or *roles,* which describe things that people do in aggre-

[5] Kenneth D. Benne and Paul Sheats, "Functional Roles of Group Members," *Journal of Social Issues* 4, 2:41-49. See also John R. Gibb and Lorraine M. Gibb, eds., "Spotlight on Member Roles," *Adult Leadership* 1, 8:2-23.

gates or groups in order to get the job done (or, sometimes, in order to *prevent* the job from getting done). To avoid confusion over these three terms, which are sometimes used synonymously, they may be defined as follows:

| | |
|---|---|
| Behaviors | actions of individual group members expressed in verbal and/or nonverbal terms. |
| Functions | behaviors directed purposefully toward building the group and toward helping it accomplish its task (e.g., harmonizing is a behavior which can be called a function since it implies intent to affect the building of the group). |
| Roles | characteristic playing of certain sets of functions by group members. |

For the purposes of this discussion, the term *functions,* as defined above, will be used.

## Task Functions

With the development over the years of what might be called the American "Cult of Efficiency,"[6] there is great individual anxiety in aggregates over the possibility of wasting time. Thus, the members of a typical committee called for the purpose of accomplishing a certain task rarely take time to get to know each other or to deal with its process level in any way. They are much too intent on making decisions and taking quick action. In getting the work done, one or more of the members must contribute behaviors that can be termed *task functions.* Some of these are:

1. *Initiating:* stating or defining the group task, stating goals, suggesting action, proposing plans, supplying ideas for the accomplishment of the task, making suggestions for the use of resources.

2. *Supplying Information:* giving facts, providing data relevant to the concerns of group.

---

[6] For a treatment of researches that moved out of the "efficiency expert" approach in industry and into a human relations framework to increase worker output see F. J. Roethlisberger and W. J. Dickson, *Management and the Worker* (Cambridge, Mass.: Harvard University Press, 1939).

3. *Giving Opinion:* stating feelings as to the workability of plans, giving ideas as to whether they may or may not be accepted.

4. *Requesting Information:* Identifying areas where facts and concepts are needed, asking for suggestions and ideas.

5. *Providing Resources:* Listing possible resource people or materials, bringing in solutions developed in other places, using one's own background and expertise.

6. *Requesting Opinion:* calling for member expression of feeling about procedures or ideas, asking for acceptance or rejection of objectives or proposals.

7. *Clarifying:* restating ideas of others in one's own terms, questioning proposals, interpreting.

8. *Elaborating:* building on ideas of others, restating one's own ideas in more complex form.

9. *Summarizing:* restating main ideas proposed at any point, combining ideas of others in single form.

10. *Consensus Testing:* stating conclusion or decision and asking for group commitment, calling for vote of general agreement.

11. *Orienting:* reminding group of deadlines, keeping minutes, keeping discussion relevant and on track.

## Maintenance Functions

While the supplying of task functions by the leader and/or members should lead to effective task accomplishment, it does not always succeed, and quite often the work of the members is slow and inefficient. Such blocks to progress and member satisfaction are common in an aggregate where the social needs of members are ignored. What seems needed are behaviors that act to build more of a group feeling—and intragroup respect and rapport. Such group building maintenance functions are:

1. *Recognizing:* use of names in group discussion, giving of credit for good ideas or actions, supporting, encouraging.

2. *Accepting:* expressions of friendliness and warmth, smiling and head nodding, indicating that one's absence is regretted and that one's presence is noted and welcome.

3. *Harmonizing:* helping others to understand the basis of their disagreements, reconciling conflicts, helping members to see the other fellow's point.

4. *Compromising:* helping others to combine their ideas into a mutually satisfactory proposal, giving ground on one's position in favor of a more generally acceptable statement, giving consent or commitment to an experimental tryout of a not yet personally acceptable idea.

5. *Norm Testing:* trying out procedures seemingly agreed upon by the group to find out if they are really acceptable.

6. *Communication Facilitating:* helping others to participate, making process-level comments, exploring personal feelings, voicing perceptions of the group feeling.

## Individual Roles

A collection of people can become an effective group if they provide behaviors that meet both work and emotional needs of the members. The provided behaviors, in the form of task and maintenance functions, can result in sharing of leadership and responsibility by each individual member. Or the aggregate can behave in such a way as to remain an aggregate from session to session. When this happens, the submerged and unmet needs of members often lead to the playing of individual roles such as those detailed on page 74.

It is easy enough to scorn these individual roles and to condemn those who play them. What is more difficult, but more helpful, is to raise questions about the *process* of a group, which makes such role playing necessary for some individuals.

If these role descriptions are realistic, if such behaviors *do* occur in aggregates or groups—they certainly can prevent the accomplishment of any task such as learning. The teacher can use the big stick of institutional authority to suppress these symptoms of group malfunction, *or he can use them as potential learning experiences.* More and more evidence is piling up in American schools that suppression is not working. Perhaps teachers ought to try some alternative approaches.

To deal constructively with the malfunction caused by individual roles, the group needs to create an atmosphere in which it can look searchingly at its process level the way it now looks at its content level. Always remembering that the player of the individual role is a member of the group, group members need to project more acceptance and understanding of its members. By playing an individual role, the person so behaving is proclaiming his needs without stating them in words. The sad part about the communication is that his behavior, in an uncaring aggregate, usually succeeds in doing just the opposite of what he wants. What can be done?

As the material on page 74 suggests, each of these members playing individual roles have potential value for the group. If the group can respond to them in a helpful, non-punitive way, they may be able to meet their individual needs without resorting to these roles which block the group in its operation. On their parts, the individuals must make an effort to learn more effective behavior.

The Dictator needs to learn that his forceful leadership will be more acceptable if he stops pushing it down people's throats and that the resistance of others is not based on rejection of his ideas but rather on his methods. The Prize Fighter needs to learn that action is good, but that purposeless conflict is just plain annoying. He might help himself by thinking through his purposes and getting action started in more appropriate ways. The Playboy needs to be more selective in his efforts at joking and to see more clearly the difference between humor and silliness. The Apple Shiner and the Point Picker need to use their abilities in more constructive ways and develop the self-confidence to try other necessary group functions when they are needed. The Martian Observer and the Marble Taker need group acceptance and support very badly, but they also need to reward those who do try to help by moving, even slightly, away from their rigid positions of withdrawal.

## Interaction in the Classroom

As noted on pages 55-56 above the peer culture in the schools is certainly a force not only to be reckoned with but to be mined constantly for educative experiences. Students who are helped to identify, understand, and improve their own values and the behavior stemming from these values will not only be more motivated and functional in the present class—they will

| Individual Role | Behavior | Need | Potential Value |
|---|---|---|---|
| Dictator | dominates, does not listen, exerts strong pressure using fast talk, loud voice, sarcasm | to be seen as group leader | takes position, establishes direction |
| Prize Fighter | argues, criticizes, picks fights, encourages others to fight | to get the action started | keeps things lively, provokes group action |
| Playboy | treats all discussion as source of hilarity, makes inappropriate jokes, mocks serious proposals | to demonstrate humor and superiority | relieves tension, makes people laugh |
| Apple Shiner | supports everything teacher says, sides with dictators, never makes waves | to be accepted, particularly by dominant group figures | provider of support and encouragement as well as recognition |
| Point Picker | takes issue with everything anyone says, never really agrees or gives consent to a group decision | to be seen as thoughtful intellectual | Devil's advocate. Loyal opposition, calls for careful examination of all sides of question |
| Martian Observer | sits silently, answers direct questions with terse comments and returns to silence | to avoid being revealed as inadequate | provides the group with a question as to the effects of its process, can make the group proud and close by finally participating |
| Marble Taker | withdraws into silence after ideas have been challenged or ignored | to be appreciated by others | also challenges the aggregate to become more sensitive as a group |

be more effective future citizens in a world suffering from ineffective behavior in the face of crisis.

The teacher himself, of course, could have benefited by exposure to such teaching. The more he (you) place(s) himself (yourself) in charge of and control of everything that goes on, the more he (you) give(s) evidence of inexperience in group norm setting. Such inexperience leaves the teacher pitted against the class in a win-lose situation where no one can really win. Each year, many teachers lose this unnecessary battle and leave teaching or stay to continue losing. And, each year the more aggressive of these teacher-battlers win the battle for order at the expense of student dignity and self-direction.

In an interesting collection of readings for teachers, Johnston presents an article by James Herndon describing a class in a predominantly black San Francisco school. These youngsters are in a constant struggle—a losing one for both students and teachers—to gain some control of their own experience. Herndon's approach, in this situation is different from most of his fellow teachers of whom he says,

> They know certain ways to get control of the class, although even these didn't work consistently because the kids were not easily threatened, having little to lose. The material which was so important, which had to be "covered" once order was established, was supposed to lead toward specific understanding and broader knowledge. But actually what was happening was that teachers were presenting the students, every day, with something for them either to do or not do, while keeping them through "order" from any other alternative.[7]

It is not Herndon's nor the present author's purpose to destructively criticize teachers. Rather, it is to point up the defects in a teacher-directed approach which allows little or no room for student-to-student or student-to-teacher input in group norm formation. The classroom aggregate will not make progress under the direction of a despot—even a benevolent one. Some teacher-despots use manipulative charm to gain their preplanned ends while others let threats and force show through in a more naked way. The non-despot says to the class, in effect, there

[7] Bernard Johnston, *The Literature of Learning* (New York: Holt, Rinehart and Winston, Inc., 1971), p. 161.

are certain givens in our situation such as my being the appointed rather than elected leader, our contract to be in this place during certain times on certain days, the obligation to deal with certain subject matter, the obligation to report data such as attendance and grades, and the necessity to keep our activities from interfering with those of other members of the school community. Within these, and perhaps a few more, boundaries we should be free to set up the norms and activities of our little society (this class) in whatever way *we* think best.

The crucial question here is *not* norm setting or activity selection—it is teacher stance. *Any* aggregate (any class) is faced with the task of developing its norms and deciding on its activities. The question raised here is *who shall do it*? This, in itself, begins to develop a norm. When the teacher preplans and tells the students what to do, this is the suggestion of a norm of teacher direction. Any aggregation of students, used to such a norm and *used to accepting such a norm*, will move into a support position. The difficulties referred to by Herndon happen only when the students resist the norm, and the teacher moves in forcefully to knock out the resistance. Difficulties of a different sort, of course, can occur when the student expectation is to be told what to do and the teacher resists by demanding that they plan together or that the students, on their own, make decisions about activities.

In short, norm development cannot be avoided as any collection of people sit down to work together. The notion presented here (in itself a challenge to norms of teacher direction) is that both teacher and students get actively and openly involved in deciding how they will behave in this learning situation and to what process of inquiry they will apply themselves.

Another, and very important part of this process, is that norms are always open to testing, questioning, and proposals for change. Hand-raising (at least by students) to gain attention is a typical norm. As it is tested in the classroom, it may seem an unnecessary part of some activities. If so, the teacher—or a student—might propose that the class try just speaking out without raising hands first. If everyone agrees, this new norm can be tested, refined, adopted, or rejected. One outgrowth might be a feeling that seating be changed so that everyone can see everyone else. Raising hands is most appropriate where the teacher does most of the talking to students seated one behind the other in rows. This norm also places control and traffic direction squarely in the hands of the teacher. If it is deemed desirable that *both* teacher *and* students share control and direction, this is a norm change and other norms will probably have to follow suit. Many classroom discussions are carried out with students seated in rows and the teacher standing at the front of the room. Discussion conducted with such physical arrangements is certainly possible, but it is also somewhat awkward and inhibiting to student-student interaction. If a discussion is really desired, it would be much more sensible to seat people in a circle.

Circling, squaring, or rowing students in a classroom, however, is not the main question in group development. The main question is whether norms can be set or questioned by anyone besides the teacher. A group-centered teacher who felt strongly about seating the class in a circle would also check this proposal with the students. Since they are more than likely accustomed to row seating, they may not favor a circle. The *decision*, then, would rest not with the teacher alone, but with the class *including the teacher*. Possible decisions might be (1) do it anyway, (2) leave the seats in rows, or (3) try out the circle seating with the option of abandoning it if it does not seem to be more helpful than row seating.

For the reader who may, at this point, be having a little trouble with terms such as *aggregate, group, group development, group-centered teaching, teacher-centered teaching, norms,* and *activities* should refer to the section, "Definition of Terms," on pages 5-8, which treats aggregates and groups and pages 42-51 which treat teacher-centered and group-centered teaching.

Aggregates interact on a formal non-trusting level allowing little or no expression of feeling as to what is going on. This way of interacting is, in itself, a norm (accepted, expected way of behaving). As an aggregate exists through time, all members begin to know better what they can expect of each other's behavior. They begin to support old norms with which they entered this new situation or they begin to develop new ones or to combine some of the old with some new. These things happen while the aggregate proceeds together through a series of learning experiences. Such learnings cover a broader spectrum than that which is openly dealt with in the class. While some reading or arithmetic or English may be learned, many other things are surely going on. The teacher is learning to be more at ease in the classroom or, perhaps, less at ease; to be more or less effective in motivating students and controlling their behavior; and/or to like or dislike students in general or certain students in particular. Students, on their part, may be learning to be more self-directing or more dependent, and they may be learning clever ways to lure Mr. Jones into bypaths about his war experiences or to send Miss Smith out of the room in tears. Both teacher and students develop feelings about each other and about what they are doing. These feelings do get expressed one way or the other—directly or indirectly. If direct expression is blocked by a norm which insists that only subject matter may be discussed, the feelings come out in sarcasm, yelling, and seat changing by the teacher and in restlessness, inattention, open defiance, or less open "fooling around" by the students. If, on the other hand, direct expression of feeling is encouraged and students are helped to express even negative feelings in helpful rather than destructive ways, the aggregate begins to mature as a group.

No teacher can keep feelings from occurring in himself or in his students. His only choice is what norms of interaction he will demand or support in his classroom. If he is teacher-centered, he will want to run the show, he will concentrate on subject matter, and he will declare open expressions of feeling inappropriate to the classroom situation. This approach will maintain the aggregate condition and deny self-direction and affective education to students.

If he is group-centered, on the other hand, he will allow students to cooperate with him in running the show within the limits set by his superiors, he will concentrate on *both* subject matter and student discussion and decision-making skills, and he will declare open expression of feelings to be as important to the classroom situation as open expression of facts and concepts. This approach will help the aggregate to mature as a group and enhance learning in self-direction and affect education.

## Teacher-Centered Approach

Defenders of the teacher-dominated classroom—and these may very well include students—tend to stress three arguments.

First, they say, the teacher is more mature and much more expert in the subject matter than students. It is, therefore, natural that he would assume the bulk of the responsibility for planning, initiating, carrying out, and evaluating the learning activities of the class. Second, there has to be control. The teacher's superior maturity and commitment to the norms of society and the school make him the logical choice for behavioral norm-setter and enforcer. Third, teachers are by no means the ogres that their critics make them out to be. On the contrary, they tend to smile rather than frown, request rather than order, and maintain discipline with firm assurance rather than uncontrolled yelling. The modern teacher, then, is a pleasant, but firm, mature subject-matter specialist who strives always for a congenial, though well-controlled, class atmosphere in which his plans for student learning can be carried out.

Actually, the description in the paragraph above is a picture of the best the traditional school has to offer. All of us can remember teachers who fit this mold, and we remember them usually with respect and often with affection. If this is true, why would anyone be critical of a teacher-centered approach? The simplest answer is that the defenders are concentrating on approach without reviewing the outcomes of the approach. Modern and effective techniques for driving a horse and buggy do not alter the fact that it is a horse and buggy in an age of jet aircraft and high-powered automobiles. After all the arguments for teacher domination are carefully laid out, the fact remains that, at its best, it does not do the job of turning out self-directed people who can deal with feelings as well as facts.

As one examines the roots of teacher domination, one is struck with the stubborn fact that, even in its most sugar-coated manifestation, it is based on fear. Fearful people react to challenge with panic and brute force. Let the pleasantly firm teacher of the description above be challenged by students who refuse to play his game, and the iron hand comes rapidly out of the velvet glove in the form of physical force, raised voice, and expulsion from the classroom and the school. A less fearful educator would meet challenges openly with an exploration of issues and a group decision which includes student as well as teacher inputs. But fear breeds dogmatism under stress. Commenting on teacher feelings of competence, Bernard says, ". . . one does not need to resort to dogmatism if he is confident of his own competence. . . . feeling sure of oneself instills a confidence that makes it possible to respect difficult views and challenging counterstatements."[8] Educators, however, sometimes seem to lack confidence in themselves and in their students. Roots of such fear would include:

1. Fear of ridicule: High degree of teacher control would allow teacher to stay within areas of his own security. Allowing students to move into subject areas of their own interest might force the teacher to deal with items in which he is insecure and even reveal some of his ignorance.

2. Fear of control loss: If the teacher sincerely moves toward sharing the class norm-setting and direction with students, they may go through a period of confusion, "waste time," and even "make noise."

3. Fear of openly expressed feelings: Since the affect education of his students is no better than his own, expression of feeling could be hurtful. Teacher security lies in maintaining a situation in which he can express his feelings, but the students cannot. His expression is "for their own good." Their expression of feeling is "insolence."

4. Fear of student immaturity: Students are not ready to share in the direction of their learning experience. Given such freedom, they would only make a mess of it, and they would abuse the freedom by becoming "behavior problems." Far better for the teacher "who knows what is best" to set the stage and produce the play.

5. Fear of not covering the ground: This group development stuff done through permissive teaching is all well and good, but it sounds time-consuming. In this history course, we have to get from Lief Erickson to the Nixon Administration, and there is no time for frills and fads.

Such fears have, in the past, undergirded a rigid approach in the classroom which, while presented in a pleasant way, prevents students from learning to deal effectively with freedom and emotions. Since learnings in these areas are as important as any other learnings the school has to offer, it will be the task of

[8] Harold W. Bernard, *Mental Health in the Classroom* (New York: McGraw-Hill Book Co., 1970), p. 144.

present and future teachers to pioneer new ways of teaching. Their job—in cooperation with their students—will be to accomplish these ends without justifying the fears listed above. Student self-direction and affect education can and should be arrived at without producing severe teacher insecurity, chaos in the classroom, bruised feelings, student abuse of freedom, or failure to communicate necessary facts, concepts, and skills involved in subject matter.

## Group-Centered Approach

Proponents of the group-centered approach in the classroom— or in business and industry where such ideas have been explored for well over a generation—tend to stress three arguments. First, they say, whenever human beings get together—as in a classroom—they generate interpersonal feelings as well as intellectual responses to facts and concepts. If this is true, then denying open expression of feelings is as harmful to learning as it would be to prohibit any talking about mathematics in the mathematics classroom. Communication improvement—and this is what teaching and learning is all about—comes by setting a norm to deal with facts or feelings whenever one or the other seems important to the group. Second, feelings can be brought out in the open productively as group members learn skills in dealing with emotions. Rather than backing away, denying, or game-playing, people who have become a group are able to bring out feelings frankly, get support and advice from other members, *and work to resolve negative feelings where they exist.* Such resolution brings further group cohesion and mutual trust under which conditions communication is most clear and undistorted. Third, people—*including students*—can be trusted to be self-directing, self-motivating, and self-disciplining when given the chance to share leadership and to have some control of their own norm-setting and learning activities. While sharing the power and responsibilities of leadership may be difficult at first for those who have been conditioned to be passive and dependent, people *can* learn to function in a participative, democratic way with guidance from their teacher. Learning democratic behavior, and using it, will not occur in one hour or one week, but then neither will the learning of reading or writing or mathematics.

Group-centered teachers have strong commitments to scholarship, subject matter, and ground-to-be-covered. Where they part company from more directive teachers is in their belief that students must "buy in" to whatever is proposed as means and ends in the class. In addition to his own expertise, the group-centered teacher realizes that each student brings a wealth of background, needs, and interests and that the teacher's job is to help students express these three elements and, together with the teacher, build learning experiences around them.

Such a teacher begins his class with getting-to-know-each-other activities, includes himself as someone to know, and puts out his personal aims and values for the course with a view toward getting student reactions and alternative proposals. Thus, early in the class' life together, he begins to suggest norms and to seek student input in their formation. As feelings occur to him, he expresses them to the class, thus modeling the behavior of expressing feelings. As the class begins to make some tentative decisions and to implement them, the group begins to form with norms of shared leadership in dealing with both facts and feelings.

Group formation means that the aggregate (or infant group) is beginning to mature. This maturity is reflected in an increase of teacher-student and student-student dialogue in the development, questioning, testing, and development of group norms, and in the shift from teacher-dominated to group-directed activities. As a most significant group member, the teacher's expertise in subject matter and other areas is put to use both because he suggests areas and methods of inquiry *and* because students use him as a resource in helping them get to where *they* want to go.

Many group decisions in the classroom may be identical to decisions that the teacher could have made on his own, using his knowledge of psychology and subject matter. One might, therefore, question the time taken to help the class aggregate become a group. Three answers to such a question immediately suggest themselves: First, there is the motivation which comes from having made the decision themselves. Action on the decision becomes *their* action rather than the teacher's. Second, having spent time in exploring the issues on which the final decision is based, the students understand more clearly *why* they are doing what they are doing. Far too much schoolwork goes on with ultimate objectives residing only in the head of the teacher—and even the teacher may not have them stated in precise terms. Third, the group's decision is very probably similar to *but not identical* with the teacher's, and the difference, even if slight, may greatly improve the original plan. It certainly will improve it in the eyes of the learners who have worked to develop it.

A few brief illustrations of group-centered teaching may be helpful at this point:

FIRST GRADE: Miss Jones would like change in two areas. First, following their seat work, her students may spend up to forty minutes on individual interests. She is not satisfied that this individual work is serious enough for many students, and others are beginning to become bored and "fool around." Second, she has two students who will not finish even their seat work without constant attention from her. She has told the class as a whole that their individual work ought to result in longer range projects, and she has asked two bright students to work with the two dependent ones. Neither of these efforts has made much change in the direction she feels is important.

On one Monday, she announces that they will discuss the individual work tomorrow and asks that they think about why they like it and why they dislike it. On Tuesday, following the individual work, she seats them in a circle and reasks the questions. During the twenty minutes of discussion, not much is accomplished, though a few students state that the work is fun and one says it is not so much fun.

On Wednesday, she repeats the discussion, and this time more students participate. On Thursday, students are looking forward to the discussion, and many ideas come out. She lists these ideas on newsprint and tapes it on the side of the room. On Friday, with a great deal of excitement and participation, the class goes over the list and makes a decision to form quartets both for seat work and individual interests because they say that some of their classmates suggest things that they would not have thought of.

On the following Monday, Miss Jones reminds the students of their decision and allows them to select their own groups. Each group must finish seat work as a group before going on to individual interests.

*Results:*  1.  Noise level is higher, but good peer learning seems to be going on with students helping students, and there is some student effort to keep noise down.

2. The two dependent students call on the teacher only once rather than three or four times, and one of them begins to talk to his three fellow students to ask for help.

3. As each quartet finishes seat work, they move to another part of the room to share interests. Most of them begin to work on projects before the end of the allotted time.

4. Miss Jones feels better about the results than she did of results of previous efforts. Those things she feels could be improved and those things of which she disapproves (noise for one) she shares in the discussion which has now become a class norm. The class is learning discussion skills, and they have a number of new ideas which are listed on newsprint for further discussion.

FIFTH GRADE: Mr. Johnson has decided to use student committees this year to investigate, write up investigations, and report back to the rest of the class. As preparation, he analyzed a period of history into five parts, assigned each student to a committee of five, and gave each committee one of the parts to work on.

In the beginning of the group work there was much confusion and "fooling around." Students were not sure just what they were supposed to be doing, and two or three in each committee ended by doing most of the work. While the reports were read, Mr. Johnson had to break in from time to time to keep order in the class or to help the committees by asking probing questions. At one point, as he developed a topic, the class shifted to him as the leader rather than the committee that sat at the front of the room. He was the sole evaluator of the committee work, and those students in each committee who had done the bulk of the work were somewhat upset that *all* members would get the same grade.

When all committees had reported, Mr. Johnson had students write unsigned reactions to the experience. Most were negative, asking Mr. Johnson to go back to lecturing, but some were positive on the point that committee work had given them more chance to speak than they had in normal class routine. All were negative about their committee accomplishments.

Mr. Johnson handed back the reaction sheets and led a discussion based on them. Many students were surprised to hear the few positive feelings, and some modified their original negatives to include some positives.

Mr. Johnson then asked for suggestions as to next steps. The consensus was to forget group work. Mr. Johnson said that he was willing to go along with group decision, but that he, personally, felt a sense of failure in not putting the project across successfully. He said that he, personally, would like to capitalize on the positive comments and try committees once more, perhaps with some modifications. After some discussion, the group decided to go along with Mr. Johnson's suggestion.

This time, however, the class began by reading the text and some outside materials on the next area of history to be studied. This was followed by students' choosing of committees which began their work by sharing what each individual member had read and what he thought of his reading. Then, Mr. Johnson was asked to take an hour to share what *he* thought was important about this period in history. The committees compared his lecture to their readings and, through discussion, prepared what *they* thought were three important aspects. Then, in total class discussion, the fifteen aspects (three from each committee) were modified and combined to form five areas for investigation and report. Mr. Johnson took part in the discussion, but he had only one vote in the final decision like anyone else.

As a prelude to the committee work, Mr. Johnson gave a little talk on how groups work together with full rather than partial participation. Committees were given eighty minutes a day for five days to complete their work before reporting back to the class. One hour each day was spent on committee deliberation and the final twenty minutes was devoted to a discussion of "how are we doing?"

*Results:* The second group project was seen by students as far more successful than the first.

1. Committees worked with higher commitment and participation.
2. When some committees began to work with only three out of five members it was discovered that the three "workers" had in effect, taken over and excluded the inputs of the other two and that their exclusion rather than their laziness was the reason for their lack of commitment.
3. Students reported that they learned more and felt better about what they were doing.
4. The evaluation discussions also had a higher level of student commitment and participation. As a group, the class decided that next time there should be more work on how to give the reports and that the class as a whole should evaluate committees.

TENTH GRADE: In Mr. Brown's English class he made a proposal that students read their themes aloud before the class and that members of the class then give constructive criticisms. In the "How are we doing?" session held during the last half of the period each Friday, some students who had not yet read their themes raised a question about the whole procedure. Only the teacher, they claimed, should evaluate students' work because only he was really qualified. Further discussion brought out the fact that some students felt that classmates' criticisms hurt too much and that the process was a painful one which they would like to avoid if possible.

Mr. Brown continued the discussion in the following class session on Monday, asking if there were any possible alternatives to continuing or discontinuing the critiques. Some students felt that backing off would be "copping out." Others felt that, though sometimes painful, the criticisms were helpful. A suggestion was made and adopted that the themes be prepared in a two-step design. First, students would form groups of five by their own choice, and, one at a time, read their themes to only the other four who would discuss their reactions and then give a critique. The reader would then react both as to how helpful the critique seemed and also how he felt about receiving it. This would be followed by a written revision before the theme was read to the entire class which would first write a brief reaction and then discuss the theme. The reader would get both the oral and written feedback.

*Results:*   1.   Student motivation to write and to discuss themes increased. Some students who reported doing a half-hearted job in the past now reported that they devoted much more time and care to the writing.

2.   Following a general reaction that the procedure, though more valuable than the first, was time-consuming, the procedure was altered to include more discussion of what good writing should be, and these discussions were held following each five themes that were read.

3.   Students reported, and were pleased with, an increase in ability to give criticism without hurting people's feelings.

4.   Students reported an increase in interpersonal knowledge. "I never knew so much before about the other people in the class. I like to go to the class because the teacher's a nice guy, but even more because the kids are easy to get along with. I feel now like I could say almost anything in this class and nobody would mock me out. This isn't true in other classes because we never take the time to know each other."

5.   Some students are still not completely satisfied. "I usually like the teacher to make decisions because I

don't trust the kids. But one good thing here is that I can talk out, and if I get support I can change things. I think I'm going to be more active in future."

6. The teacher is especially pleased that the students themselves, without his help (he never thought of it), decided on discussions of what good writing is. Many nonparticipating students whom he tried personally to reach and failed are now getting involved because of the excitement of their classmates and because *the members of the class are now taking responsibility for bringing in nonparticipators in helpful ways rather than nagging or embarrassing ways.*

These are some ways in which group-centered teachers function in the classroom. They do not neglect their personal responsibilities as leaders appointed by the school. Rather, they maintain their roles as expert resources while seeking to help students help themselves and their classmates. The group-centered teacher considers *all* members of the group to have great untapped potential for participating in their own learning and that of their classmates. Such a teacher does not force *his* ideas as the only ones that are really worthwhile. *He does not even try to sell them.* What he *does* do is offer himself as a special group member and a special resource not only in subject matter but in communication. He is willing to share his personal feelings as to what is going on as well as to request that students do the same. He is also willing to test out ideas which seem important to the group by allowing them to try things even when he feels that they will not work out. He has faith that if he offers himself sincerely and authentically, the group-as-group will follow suit and become self-directing and self-controlling.

## Group Training for the Teacher

Schools of education are increasingly getting into interaction analysis and sensitivity training for preservice teachers. Teachers already in service can read books like this one and those in the suggested readings, and they can go back to college or mount in-service programs that will help them to see themselves more clearly in terms of how their behavior affects others and help them to a greater sophistication in group communication techniques.

Interaction analysis[9] refers to the efforts of communication researchers to codify types of verbal and nonverbal behaviors occurring in classrooms and to chart the flow of communicative behaviors in any specific situation so that the kind of interaction going on can be clearly seen. As a tool, interaction analysis is valuable feedback material in establishing the types and frequencies of teacher-pupil-pupil activities and behaviors. Authoritarian teachers input 70 to 80 percent of the total classroom verbalizations, and their talk is more likely to be directing, correcting, and scolding than supporting, encouraging, and focused on bringing out feelings.

It would be most helpful to the self-improving teacher if he could videotape, or at least audiotape, one of his class sessions and apply some system of interaction analysis to get an idea of what he is really doing in the classroom. The reader might attempt such a project, asking questions such as: Am I talking far too much? Am I locked into a recitation method where I am the only one asking questions while scattered students respond with brief, narrow, factual answers? Do I ask questions that call not for facts but for analysis, synthesis, or problem solving *based* on facts? Is my communication pattern: teacher to John, back to teacher to Mary, back to teacher to Fred, and so on—or do I encourage and structure student-to-student interaction by throwing the student response to me back to the rest of the students? Do my students prove their learning of facts only by giving answers in response to a kind of verbal completion test conducted by me or do they prove learning by using the facts to develop further questions of their own?

Study of interaction analysis, in which every teacher should engage, should do more than help educators to see clearly what they are doing in the classrooms. It should provide them with mature, intelligent responses to the authoritarian-permissive controversy. If we wish to improve the quality of teaching, we should avoid traps such as nasty teacher versus nice teacher, overcontrolling versus do-as-you-please, or silent-frightened "discipline" versus anarchy and mob rule. Instead of dealing with highly abstract labels like authoritarian and permissive

[9] See pp. 110-123 of this book.

(the overuse of which proves that our teachers failed to teach us to think effectively), we would make better use of our time by looking at our objectives. Do we wish to turn out a student product who is dependent on someone in authority to do most of the thinking or do we wish to develop a student who can think for himself? Do we wish to keep students dependent on authority for control, or do we wish to help students to develop self-control? Do we wish passive or active learners, and how do we define *these* terms? Do we wish to teach bunches of facts or processes of inquiry?

Analysis of classroom verbal interaction can help us to see more clearly just what is going on. It can also help us to formulate more clearly what we wish would go on in terms of the objectives we have set. If it is the teacher's intent to carry on a discussion and to encourage student self-direction, an analysis of verbal interaction can pinpoint where he is succeeding and where he is failing. Too many teachers talk far too much in what they are calling a class discussion, but telling them that they are dominating is too abstract to be helpful. It is not enough for the teacher merely to talk less. He could talk less and still dominate the discussion, or he could talk less and leave the students puzzled as to what to do with the sudden silence. On the other hand, the students might fill in the silence by talking more, but they might not say anything that would help them learn. It is not merely amount of talk that is significant—quality also must be analyzed.

The author once visited a teacher who was very proud of the amount of student participation in his classes. As he enthusiastically fired a number of questions calling for short, factual responses, most hands would go up and one lucky student after another would be called upon to respond. Analysis of the session showed two things. On the content level, the teacher did almost all the thinking and questioning, communication pattern was teacher to student to teacher to student to teacher, and student response was almost completely narrowly factual. On the process level (checked by observer's response to enthusiasm, facial expression, and amount of student participation plus unsigned student written reactions to the teacher and the class) the students liked and trusted the teacher. They could freely take a chance in answering questions because the teacher rewarded them with approval even when their answers were wrong. They responded favorably to the teacher also in terms of "He knows his subject," "He's excited about what he's doing," and "He never makes you feel stupid."

This teacher, judged on many teaching criteria, was doing an excellent job. Until he examined the analysis data and spent some time studying the analysis process, however, he had never realized that he was doing most of the thinking for his students and that their study habits had become the amassing of facts in order to play this particular classroom game with success. Following his study of interaction analysis, he did not abandon his highly successful recitation exercises, but he began to include questions which forced students to express relationships between facts, build a number of facts into generalizations, and use facts to solve problems. This process soon had the students *asking questions as well as answering them*, and he began to throw their questions back to the group. As this happened, the communication pattern changed to teacher-student-student-student-teacher-student-student-student. When students were asked to react to teacher and class, they moved rapidly from unsigned sheets to open discussion. The gist of their thinking reactions was that what was now happening was more difficult for them, but it was forcing them to learn more and this was exciting. The feeling reactions repeated the positive comments about the teacher *but now included similar comments about classmates.*

This teacher was teaching facts as well as ever. But he had extended his repertoire. He was now teaching students to think and be more independent and self-directing, and he was teaching, by example, how to deal with feelings in a positive rather than a negative way. The students were moving from admiring him as a good guy to becoming good guys themselves.

Here was a strong, hard-driving, directing, well-organized, knowledgeable teacher who rarely had a "discipline problem." Yet he was able to grow even further and build a group out of an admiring aggregate, sharing some of the direction and control. It seems apparent that he had characteristics in addition to those listed above. He was, for example, able to look at himself critically; he was able to allow students to express opinions of him; and he was not afraid to give his students freedom within limits. Much of his ability to express his own feelings and to encourage others to express theirs he feels he owes to the sensitivity training in which he has engaged.

In looking at the field of affect education (sensitivity training, encounter groups, the human potential movement), one should set it within the context of any teaching-learning experience. Teachers do well with skill development in and understanding of reading, writing, mathematics, and other subjects, but teaching could be better and learners could improve as learners. This is true in affect education as it is in cognitive education. Sensitivity training is certainly no panacea for emotional problems, and some participants in this training seem to learn more than do others. Under expert leadership, however, it offers a good opportunity to get in touch with feelings and to feel less restricted and apprehensive in interactions with others. As such, it seems an excellent ingredient for classroom teacher preparation.

Sensitivity training[10] is a group communication experience designed to help people lower defenses and share perceptions of

[10]The major source book in this field has been Leland Bradford, ed., *T-Group Theory* (New York: Wiley, 1964). Other helpful readings include Gerard Egan, *Encounter: Group Processes for Interpersonal Growth* (Belmont, Calif.: Brooks/Cole Publishing Company, 1970); Arthur Burton, ed., *Encounter: The Theory and Practice of Encounter Groups* (San Francisco: Jossey-Bass Inc., 1970); and Robert W. Siroka, Ellen K. Siroka, and Gilbert A. Schloss, *Sensitivity Training and Group Encounter* (New York: Grosset and Dunlap, 1971).

Many universities and colleges provide some courses in the dynamics of groups at work, though many of these are still taught by lecture. The author's own college has recently instituted an M.A. degree program in Human Organizational Development which offers training in affect education for the classroom teacher.

Major sources of training programs include:

National Training Laboratories
National Education Association
1201 16th St. N.W.
Washington, D.C. 20036

Western Behavioral Sciences Institute
1121 Torrey Pines Road
La Jolla, California 92037

Esalen Institute
Big Sur, California 93920

each other as they would not do in the usual closed emotional climate most of us are used to in aggregates. While many lay and clinical people are highly critical of sensitivity training, other laymen and clinicians support it as "therapy for normals." It is no instant miracle cure for emotional blockages, and, in inexperienced hands, it has potential for psychological damage. However, much work has been done in the field, and sensitivity training or group encounter, in skillful hands, seems to hold great promise for helping people to be less rigid and withholding of their feelings.

Since such learning is emotional in nature, the teaching is done by laboratory method in groups of about ten or twelve led by specially trained leaders from the social and behavioral sciences. Called unstructured, the experience is really highly structured but in a different way. In the training group there is no given agenda. Participants are not told what to do or what to talk about. The leader does not lead in the usual way by structuring or telling. While different leaders have different styles, a typical group opening would begin with the leader saying, "We are here to learn something about how groups function and about the effect our behavior has on others. If these are our objectives, we might as well get started." At this point, the leader stops talking, and the participants look uncertainly around in silence that seems to last for hours. Actually, only a minute or two usually elapse before someone breaks the silence. This person might say, "Well, I don't know what we're supposed to be doing, but I don't like wasting time. Now, I have this problem in my classroom . . ." From this point, one participant after another contributes to the conversation and comes into the group. Since people are used to talking about topics when they get together, the group usually begins by trying to select a topic which everyone can get into. Gradually, they get the idea that the best topic would be themselves. The move-

---

At the local levels, university departments of social psychology are usually helpful contacts. The author's own organization is an example of a college-based service for consultation and sensitivity training programs for schools, businesses, and community organizations:

Montclair Human Resources Laboratory
Montclair State College
Upper Montclair, New Jersey 07043

ment is from self-investment to mutual trust to lowering defenses and façades. At this point, a norm of "feedback" is developed, and people give and receive feelings about each other, both positive and negative. The negative feedback is possible without hurt feelings and raising of defenses because of the mutual trust and a developing skill in expressing feelings while taking into account the readiness of the receiver to receive "feedback."

Because "feedback" is an avenue to learning that most of us seek constantly, and because "feedback" is usually withheld rather than freely given in our day-to-day interactions, the sensitivity training experience is a highly valuable one. A person leaves his group with a sense of individual and group accomplishment and keener awareness of self and others. This awareness is largely within the area of feelings—unfortunately a strange area to most people. The sense of accomplishment and job at the close of a training group is in proportion to how much one has been able to unfreeze and unwrap his feelings. A teacher in one of the author's groups summed it up at the end by saying, "This has been such fun, but it's also gone so deep. What a shame that all I learned in forty years was to deny my feelings and deny others the right to theirs. I spent the first two group sessions telling everyone in a snotty way that feelings didn't really matter. I guess I was trying to convince myself. I was so frightened- frightened even to come to this sensitivity thing. But it was so wonderful to finally admit that I had feelings. And, to my amazement, people really liked me—even without all my carefully prepared façades. Now I know what the kids mean when they say, 'Hey, wow!!' I'm not going right home and change the world because I know that most of my friends are just as frightened as I used to be of feelings though they'd never come right out and admit it. No, I'm not going out to sensitize the world, either. I'm going to be me like I've always been, but now I'm going to listen for feelings and when I hear them I'm going to respond as helpfully as I can."

Nothing, including sensitivity training, has magic, and people can reach their feelings and respond to others without specific training. A few people do well with self-teaching in the emotional area, and a few get so tied up that they need psychotherapy. For most of us in the middle ground, however, the training group can be very helpful. The training group has no magic, but magic exists, brought there by the participants. All of us have so much to bring to others, and yet we keep so much to ourselves in fear that others would reject, deny, or ignore our feelings. Sadly, in thus protecting ourselves, we reject, deny, and ignore the feelings of others.

One or two training experiences do not qualify one as a group leader, and this book does not advocate turning the classroom into a training group. What is helpful in interaction analysis and in sensitivity training is, as the teacher quoted above has said, that one can use training to be a better and more aware listener and to free oneself of the reluctance to respond to the feelings of another. Feelings, both positive and negative, *are* expressed in every classroom. *And they are responded to.* The trouble is that they are expressed and responded to so indirectly that they are never confronted and resolved. It is in helping people to more direct expression and response that teaching begins to reach toward higher levels of relevance and personal meaning. Mere presentation of facts and concepts is a most unsophisticated notion of education.

## Process and the Total Group

All of the foregoing is really restatement in behavioral terms of questions teachers have asked themselves for generations. How do I get Johnny involved in the class? How do I prevent Sam from bullying his classmates without making him resentful or withdrawn? How do I tell Mary that she doesn't have to lick my boots to get my approval? What do I do for Joan, who is getting to be the most disliked girl in the class? Probably, the only really different note struck in this book is the notion that such problems are properly those of the total group and not just the *teacher's alone.* If the teacher can teach the class how to deal with its process level as well as its content level, he may be holding the key to a rich educational experience that will not only increase learning potential but expand its base. He might begin by asking himself what is the real value of learning subject matter if one does not also increase one's ability to be a satisfied, effective human being.

# chapter 4

# Interaction Exercises

In the preceding chapter, the idea of process-level communication was developed, and it was suggested that classroom aggregates begin to communicate more on this level if they wish to mature as groups. A teacher, wishing to foster such maturity, would encourage student to student communication on the process level as well as the content level and would deal with *his* feelings as well as his thoughts in his own interaction with students. Classroom talk on the process level will never be concerned with deep, dark secrets of the soul nor should it be. What needs to be dealt with are small irritations and distortions of feelings that lead to blocks in communication on the content level. Teacher and students need the freedom to be able to say, "I'm bored," or "I felt bad when you said that." They need to say even negative things in a caring, helpful way, and they need to have enough mutual trust to deal with and resolve negative feelings rather than backing away from them. Such trust comes from interpersonal knowledge and the development of informal as well as formal relationships. For such development on the process level *without neglecting the equally important content level*, the exercises in this chapter may be used as beginnings.

Though no effort has been made to differentiate sharply between elementary and secondary school, the reader should be able to select and/or modify these approaches for his particular students. Kindergarten and primary-grade youngsters may not verbalize on the same level as high school seniors, but they share the same social needs for acceptance, achievement, and affection. And, like the seniors, they bring to school a great deal of interaction experience and attitudes that are never really tapped in many classrooms where content-level emphasis is the norm. The teacher's personal attitude and his acceptance of affective as well as cognitive needs on the part of his students will determine to a great extent whether he will use these experiences well and go on to develop others tailored to his own specific needs. This book should really be only a beginning.

Teacher stance should include the values of group formation and peer learning. His students have learned, and can learn more, from their peers and from their own individual explorations related to their present interests. The successful teacher will stress cognitive (content level) learning, but he will not fail to combine it, where appropriate, with affective (process level) learning.

Cognitively, students need to develop literacy; go on to gain an understanding of the scientific, technological, and social aspects of their culture; and begin to develop marketable skills. Affectively, they need to gain increasing data on who they are and what they are worth, to extend their social skills in meeting and getting along with others, to deal with their personal feelings in increasingly mature ways, to feel enough trust in others and confidence in self to participate freely in classroom activities, to see relevance of schooling to their present lives, to be more self-directing and self-responsible, and to have a part in setting classroom norms.

With these guidelines in mind, let us look at some ways to proceed.

## Focus on People

Any student of any age in any class comes to the first meeting with personal questions. Who am I, what will I be in this class, will teacher and students make me feel comfortable or uncomfortable, will the class be interesting or dull, what will I get out of it? The kindergartner who cries and holds on to Mother does

not know whether his needs for feeling secure an
will be met in this strange thing called a school,
had much practice in withholding expression
The college student has more knowledge in the fo
practice in the latter, but his needs are not basi
from those of the kindergartener. If this is true, it might be well
to begin a class by looking at these needs rather than jumping
right into the subject matter.

## Who Am I?—Who Are You?

A design which brings immediate needs out into the open and
begins to tap student backgrounds is a pairing exercise centered
on the questions, "Who am I?", "Who are you?", and "What
do I expect of this class?"

At the first session, after whatever housekeeping chores
that seem necessary are taken care of, the teacher begins by
modeling the behavior he is going to ask of the students. He
welcomes them, comments on the fact that they are going to
spend a great deal of time together during the year ahead, and
suggests that whatever good or bad lies in the experience will
come from the participation—or lack of participation—of everyone present. He then goes on to introduce himself not only
with facts about himself (content level) but with statements
about the kind of person he is and how positively and negatively
he reacts to certain student behaviors. Finally, he states briefly
some of the content-level and process-level expectations he has
about this class. (At this point, he can do all this without intro-
ducting terms like communication, content level, or process
level, or he can do a small lecturette, using the chalkboard to
teach terms that can be referred to later.)

Having finished his response to the three questions, he says
that he is sure that the students have thought about them, too.
And if they are to work together during the year, forming a
miniature community for the purpose of learning, they might
well begin by getting to know some of their classmates. As a
start, they can pair up with someone they do not already know
or would like to know better. Subject of conversation would
be telling something about oneself, getting to know more about
the other, and sharing expectations about the future of the

Following the pairs, students would move into quartets, d finally into a general class discussion.

The general flow of this exercise is as follows:

*Good idea*

| Time | Activity |
|---|---|
| 0- 5 minutes | Teacher introduces self. |
| 5-10 minutes | Students walk around saying hello, select a partner, and sit down again in pairs. |
| 10-15 minutes | Pairs respond to each other in terms of Who am I? Who are you? What do I expect from this class? |
| 15-25 minutes | Pairs join other pairs to form quartets, introduce each other, and share the data from the pairs. |
| 25-45 minutes | Teacher ends quartets and conducts general class discussion on expectations. |
| 45-50 minutes | Student writing of reactions to exercise. |

Notes:

1. Since this is probably an unusual experience for students, the teacher should expect some confusion and even some giggling nervousness. This will pass in time as the students learn to deal more effectively with this new norm.
2. During the pairs and quartets, the teacher can join in, walk around the room getting a sense of what is going on, or remain at the front of the room where he began.
3. The discussion does not need to be recorded or have its main points listed on the board. Teacher should throw comments back to the class for further questioning and amplification. Purpose of discussion is to get students to voice their feelings and to explore further the various points brought up. Negative feelings should be encouraged and explored if they are voiced, including those of the teacher.
4. A teacher-prepared reaction sheet should be responded to by students following discussion. No signature required. Items should include: (1) circle a number from one to ten reflecting evaluation of session (low numbers, poor; high numbers, excellent), (2) written explanation of number circled, and (3) listing of the three most important points in discussion.
5. The teacher can collect the sheets and use them in planning the next session or he can turn them over to

a student committee and have them plan. In any event, the data should be fed back to the class.

## Sharing

Just as athletes are trained to do warm-up exercises before playing a game, learning groups should warm up before beginning to work. The aim in learning group warm-ups should be increasing interpersonal knowledge and rapport. The following exercises should be helpful for the teacher who can use them as they are, adapt them, or invent others for his particular class and age group.

**Clean your pockets.** Boys' pockets and girls' pocketbooks contain a host of treasures having personal meaning for them. Capitalizing on this, the teacher can have the students sit in groups of four to six, share with each other some of the things they usually carry around with them, and talk about the meaning to them of the various items.

**Bring something precious.** A variation of the clean-pockets exercise is one in which students (and the teacher) plan to bring something to a particular session of the class. This something should be an item that has a great deal of personal meaning to them. This exercise allows even the most shy member of the class to present himself or herself to the others. Besides the sheer fun of this exercise, one valuable result is that many nonparticipators gain enough peer support to begin participating more actively in the regular activities of the class.

**Gift-giving.** This exercise is an extension of the occasional practice of bringing gifts for a class grab bag. The directions here are to bring something to class that would fill a need for or be particularly appropriate for one other member. For subgroups of four or five, the directions might be to bring something for each of the members. The gift should be symbolic and perhaps homemade to avoid putting financial burdens on students. What is being asked is a personal statement. Both giver and receiver should discuss the meanings involved. This exercise is most helpful in building a good group atmosphere.

## Focus on Projects

While the people-centered aspects of group building are important—and too often overlooked in the classroom—the task-centered aspects are also quite necessary ingredients. Responsibilities of teacher and students include planning, carrying out, and evaluating learning experiences in the content as well as the process areas. Members need to get to know each other better, but they also need to work together to accomplish classroom-centered tasks. The following exercises combine the two by having students work on tasks *and then look at their process level.*

### Visual Reports

This exercise is designed to further the content and process skills of committees which have already begun to work well as teams. The teacher states that discussion and report writing are two good ways of sharing learning and perhaps learning more. A third way is visual reporting in which a group constructs a bulletin-board display, a working model, or some other physical thing which represents a summation of their investigation of subject matter. Such constructions could include a student-made alphabet chart, a model of the town in which the students live, drawings of life on the American frontier, an illustration of the human body with acetate overlays of vital organs and systems, or a teaching machine which teaches long division. The author once asked a seventh-grade English class to sum up two months of their work. After much discussion, they decided that learnings lay in reading, writing, speaking, and listening. Four seven-student committees then selected one of these areas apiece; carefully reviewed what had been taught and learned to date; made two-dimensional representations in words, diagrams, and drawings; covered an entire wall with wrapping paper; and created a composite class mural.

While determination of what is to be done, and preparation

for doing it may take hours of class time and home study, the actual exercise should not take more than one or two class sessions. The construction of the visual report (content level) should be discussed and evaluated, *and* the behavior of the group-as-a-whole while doing the project (process level) should also be discussed and evaluated. The flow would be as follows:

| *Time* | *Activity* |
| --- | --- |
| 0- 5 minutes | Teacher reminds class that the activity has two parts. They will evaluate themselves on the quality of the visual report and also on the way they work as a group. |
| 5-25 minutes | Subgroups go to work assembling the materials they have brought to class. |
| 25-30 minutes | Teacher calls a halt to the work, and students discuss how they feel about the participation or lack of participation of subgroup members. Does everyone feel included or are some left out? Does any change need to be made in their process? |
| 30-40 minutes | Subgroups resume work on visual report. |
| 40-45 minutes | Subgroups sum up the *content* and *process* parts of their work. How is the report now that we have done it? How well did we manage to work as a team? |

Notes:
1. Subgroups will do most of their preparation before the exercise session. To that session they will bring all necessary materials to be assembled and have finishing touches put to them.
2. Groups will self-evaluate and give themselves a grade for the work.
3. Following the exercise, time should be provided for the subgroups to explain their construction and answer questions from other members of the class.

## Listening-Helping Skills

One of the largest blocks to effective group work is lack of training in organizing thoughts, listening to others, elaborating ideas, and using all members of a group rather than just a few.

The following exercise gives everyone a chance to get into the act and to develop content-level as well as process-level skills.

Preparation:   After committees of three or four have isolated an area for study and have discussed ways of investigating and reporting it, each member has the homework assignment of thinking through what must be done and who will do what. On the exercise day, each boy or girl will bring along notes and be ready to explain a plan of procedure.

| *Time* | *Activity* |
|--------|-----------|
| 0- 5 minutes | Teacher asks each student to take letter A, B, C, or D in his group. A will explain his plan to B for five minutes while B tries to draw him out and clarify the ideas. Meanwhile C and D will act as observers, writing an account of the plan as they hear it. At the end of the five minutes, C and D will hand their notes to A and the whole group will have three minutes to discuss and further clarify. |

This eight-minute sequence is then repeated three times so that each person gets a chance to play each role.

| I | III |
|---|-----|
| A explains to B<br>C and D take notes | C explains to D<br>A and B take notes |

| II | IV |
|---|-----|
| B explains to C<br>D and A take notes | D explains to A<br>B and C take notes |

| Time | Activity |
|------|----------|
| 5-15 minutes | Round I |
| 15-25 minutes | Round II |
| 25-35 minutes | Round III |
| 35-45 minutes | Round IV |

Notes:  1.  To save time, the teacher explanation could be given a day previous to the exercise.

        2.  It is helpful to do an illustration exercise so that committee members get a more clear idea of what is expected in each role. One student in each group could prepare an explanation of something from a hobby, a

family activity, or a youth group. He would then take
the A role in Round I. B would then try to draw him
out and clarify while C and D take notes.

3. As each explainer is drawn out and clarified, he gains
skill in explaining. As the C and D notes are given to
him, he can see how people perceive (or mis-perceive)
what he says. The exercise forces each person to think
through his own plan, to listen closely to the plans of
others, and to have the experience of elaborating and
building upon the plans of others.

## How Are We Doing? Session

As the school year progresses and the aggregate begins to mature as a group, exchange of feelings ought to move from unsigned sheets to verbal classroom discussions. The *How Are We
Doing?* session is an important part of this movement. In addition to helping the teacher to know what he is doing right and
what he is doing wrong, these sessions allow for the expression
of feelings that may be interfering with learning. They also
help to extend the number of fully joined up, participating
members in the class. The expression of feeling, of course, must
include the teacher. Matters that bother him concerning items
such as discipline, motivation, and student participation may
be discussed at the *How Are We Doing?* session with much more
hope of resolution than the familiar teacher-bawling-out-the
class syndrome. This latter approach puts the teacher in the
role of the irate, dominating parent scolding the nasty little
kids. The HAWD session, on the other hand, casts the teacher
*and* the students in the roles of responsible, concerned persons
looking at a problem from many angles with a view toward
resolving it.

Though the HAWD session can be approached in a number
of ways, one effective method is as follows:

Preparation:    The HAWD session should be run by a student committee of three. This moves the teacher out of the
dominating position and frees him to participate for
himself as a group member. The day before the session, each student—and the teacher—should turn in a
brief reaction sheet to the committee which will use

the sheets to develop an agenda of items for discussion. (For each HAWD session, a different trio of students should have the responsibility for conducting the meeting.)

| Time | Activity |
| --- | --- |
| 0-15 minutes | Committee calls session to order, and one member lists on the chalkboard items that appear on five or more reaction sheets. Class members can then add items that seem important to them. Items should then be arranged in order of discussion priority. |
| 15-35 minutes | Items are now open for discussion. One member of the student committee acts as secretary, listing items and whatever action may be decided upon. Another member acts as chairman. |
| 35-45 minutes | Committee members summarize and call for decision on next steps. (Can class move on from here or is further discussion needed?) If more time is felt to be needed, plans for an additional meeting are made at this point. |

Notes: 1. As was suggested above, the teacher can use this session to give his positive and negative reactions to what is going on. At the first couple of sessions, however, unless he has something very pressing, it may be wise to avoid the possibility of dominating the discussion by remaining silent. The first few HAWD sessions are learning experiences for the students, and the teacher should let them struggle to make them successful.

2. Chances are that agendas will not be crowded and that items can be dealt with in one session. If, however, there are many items or one or two that are time-consuming with many points of view being expressed, the teacher should be prepared to allow additional class time.

3. If such additional time is a real problem for the teacher, this ought to be presented for group decision. The ideal situation is one in which everyone—not merely the teacher—has time anxiety. Another opportunity for learning here is time management. Items of importance should be dealt with, but, on the other hand, long, boring discussions are more harmful than helpful and only a specified number of class sessions are available.

If more time is needed for an important discussion, it must be paid back in some way.

## Role Playing

In the usual sense of the term, role playing is similar in nature to stage acting. Participants are given roles—and perhaps specific instructions as to how to play them—and they act out a situation for the purpose of increasing their own insight into how such people might feel in this situation, or for the purpose of providing data for an observing group, or for both these purposes. The two exercises that follow may be used with role instructions or by allowing participants to play themselves. It is important to note that they are all designed to get at specific objectives. They should be used within the context of the regular classroom situation.

### Triple-Group Exercise

This activity may be used from the beginning of the first class session. Theory is presented *after* the experience so that the experience itself creates a readiness to understand the theory. Objectives may be stated as follows: As a result of the exercise (1) students will begin to understand the forces that block communication in classroom groups, (2) individuals will begin to express themselves more freely in the class, (3) the class, including the teacher, will begin to become closer as a group, and (4) students will develop a readiness to participate actively in course planning, course discussions, and evaluation of their learning.

The procedure is used for class groups numbering eighteen to thirty-six students. Steps in conducting the exercise are as follows:

1. Teacher begins by telling the class that since they will be spending a semester (or a year) together it would be helpful at the outset to learn something about how people work in groups. In order to begin this learning, some members of the class will do a group-work exercise while the others

will observe. In this way, three things can be accomplished:
(1) improvement of group work skills, (2) development of
effective techniques for observation of groups at work,
and (3) increased knowledge about each other and, perhaps, a more spontaneous and open atmosphere for classroom discussion.

2. Following this introduction, the teacher divides the class
into three equal groups, designating them as groups A, B,
and C. (Boys and girls may be segregated, evenly distrib-
uted, or randomly assigned in these groups.)

3. Arrange chairs in three concentric circles.

4. Pair off members of Groups A and B so that each student
in Group A has a partner in Group B.

5. Group A (*interacting*) sits in the center circle and each
member places a name tag in front of him.

6. Group B (*coaching*) sits in the second circle in such a way
that each member can see the face of his partner in Group
A.

7. Group C (*observing*) sits in the outside circle in random
order.

8. Teacher distributes instruction sheets (see pp. 110-111) to
each group, giving a few minutes for reading.

9. Teacher explains that Group C will be involved in general
observation of Group A and that Group B will observe
specific individuals in Group A. Group A will function for
twenty minutes and then break into helping pairs with
observer-partners from Group B. There will be ten minutes
for these helping pairs during which time the teacher will
chat with Group C concerning their observation of Group
A as a whole.

10. When the three groups have been seated in concentric
circles, the teacher reads aloud the instructions for the
interacting group so that all members of the class know
the task.

11. Teacher says, "I think we can begin now," and sits down.
Teacher may sit with Group A or elsewhere in the room.
He may wish to take his own notes as to who participates,
who leads, who helps the group, and who hinders it.
Teacher's role is that of *silent observer*. Initially, this will

be difficult for the teacher *and* for Group A because it departs from the usual expectation of *teacher talk-student listen.* The discovery by both the teacher and the class members that significant, effective things can go on without continual teacher domination is one of the most important parts of the exercise.

12. After initial self-consciousness, members begin to talk.

13. In twenty minutes, even though the group has not finished its talk, teacher calls "Time. You will have ten minutes to confer with your observer coaches. You will want to know how they have seen you, and they will want to know if they have been clear and helpful. Group C will meet with me. You have ten minutes, and then we will return to the interacting group."

14. Helping pairs form in different parts of the room and teacher meets with Group C off to one side or in the hall if there is not enough space. Teacher asks Group C, "What did you observe?" and group members contribute their ideas. Teacher may also make *his* comments, being careful to encourage objectivity. The purpose is *not* to place blame of any sort on dominating or silent group members, but to look at results of their behavior on the group's activities.

15. After ten minutes, teacher brings Group A together again and the interaction plus observation resumes.

16. Five minutes before close of session, teacher again calls time, and each student writes his reactions to the experience. (Time allotment is five minutes for introductions, twenty minutes for interacting group, ten minutes for helping pairs, ten minutes for reconvened group, and five minutes for written reactions. This is a total of fifty minutes.)

17. At the beginning of the second session, the teacher may wish to comment on some of the written reactions. Then Group B becomes the interacting group in the center, Group C moves in to become the observer-coach group, and Group A moves to the outer circle to be general observers. The process above is repeated.

18. In the third session, Group C is the center interacting, Group A becomes the observer-coach group, and Group B moves to the outer circle as general observers. This gives each group a chance to experience all three positions.

19. In the fourth session, the class as a whole should have time to discuss the experience and share their individual feelings about it. At this time, the teacher can, if he wishes, take advantage of the open communication to explore student feelings about the course and how they would like to proceed.

20. At the fifth session, the class should have a readiness to engage in planning activities. This might be pupil-teacher planning, or it might be the teacher's explanation of how he has planned the course.

In five sessions of the course (five fifty-minute periods) the ice has been broken, students have heard the sound of their own voices, a level of trust and openness has begun—which can have great effect on the amount and level of student contributions to his class—and everyone has a sense of the direction in which the learnings will proceed.

To avoid the complete suspension of subject-centered activities during these opening sessions, mimeographed sheets or textbook assignments may be given by the teacher to be taken up in class following the sessions devoted to the exercise.

Though there will be initial confusion in the carrying out of the exercise, students will quickly adjust to it. Aside from the obvious benefit to the communications pattern of the class, the very novelty of the approach carries its own motivation.

Any encounter between human beings should occur only after certain precautions are observed. (This, of course, would include any traditional classroom activities.) Two considerations occur in this exercise. First, the helping-pair coaching aspect should be considered. Each person in the coaching group should attempt to say things that are specific and helping when conferring with a member of the interacting group. It is difficult enough to be part of a group operating in a "fishbowl" environment without being criticized harshly by one's observer. It should be emphasized that the observer is learning how to be *helpful.* He needs to put his comments in such a way that the receiver can accept them and take them in the spirit given.

Second, the teacher must be aware of the potential being opened. If he does *not* want open communication, if he is most comfortable in the dictator role in his classroom, then perhaps he does not need such an exercise. If he does want open communication, then he must be aware of the fact that such an exercise is *only the beginning.* Full advantage will occur only if this opening is followed by free expression and evaluation throughout the course. In almost all cases, years of teacher domination will have preceded this exercise, and student self-direction and self-responsibility will not happen magically in a short time. If and when such conditions do develop, both teacher and students have an unusual and enriching experience.

The three sheets following, titled "Interacting Group," "Observer-Coach Guide," and "General Observation," are given to the students at the beginning of each session (see step #8). They serve a dual purpose. First, they instruct students in what is to begin, and, second, they allow for written reactions that are helpful for both teachers and students. The wording may be modified according to student maturity and reading level.

## Diagnostic Skill Session

While an activity such as the triple-group exercise can be used to build a readiness for interaction in the classroom, specific training in group awareness and skills needs a more specific approach. Since student working committees are often formed in the classroom, and since they are rarely helped to diagnose their problems, committee work might be a good subject for a group exercise.

One hypothetical setting for such an exercise might be a tenth-grade mathematics class with twenty-eight students. (Twenty-eight is used for the purposes of illustration. Adjustments can be made for more or for fewer students.)

Three weeks ago, this class carried out a unit using student committees, which were assigned the task of developing a way to clearly present a mathematical concept to the rest of the class. The teacher's purpose here was to motivate student inquiry into the work of the course, reasoning that students would have to apply themselves diligently to the learning in order to be able to explain the processes to others. His role was to be available as a resource to each committee as it worked. A secondary goal was student learning in terms of working with others and in verbalizing one's learning.

While worthwhile mathematical learning took place, the

*Interacting Group Instructions*

As a member of the interacting group, you have the rather rare opportunity to write the text and then read it. The text will be the sum of interactions of your group, and your reading will be your analysis of the types of behaviors that helped and of those that hindered the formation of a group by the strangers who sat down together.

You and your group have the task of finding a task to accomplish. There are really no right and wrong ideas so yours are as good as anyone else's. The only outside requirement is that you go about the job in such a way that this collection of individuals begins to become a cohesive group.

Your name _____

Your reactions to the experience in general:

Figure 7

*Observer-Coach Guide Instructions*

Your Name _____. Observer's Name _____.

You will focus on a single member of the interacting group so that you can mirror his behavior to him. Your comments will be in the form of, "As I saw you, you . . ." Your behavior in the helping pair will be directed to helping *him* to think through his own behavior in the group.

Attempt, below, to describe your observee's behavior in the group. Was he quiet, domineering, helpful to others? Did he support and/or clarify the contributions of others? Did he help the group to formulate its goals?

Attempt, below, to report, as you saw it, the effects of your observee's behavior on the other members of the group. Did they react, and if so what were reactions?

Figure 8

*General Observer Instructions*

Your Name _____. Group No. _____.

You will focus on the interaction pattern of the whole group rather than on the behavior of a specific participant. Following the interaction session, you will have opportunity to compare your findings with those of others in *your* group.

You will want to note who speaks most and least, who the leaders of the group appear to be, what behaviors seem to produce group action and satisfaction, what behaviors seem to block the group in getting at its task, and whether the group acts as an *entire* group, as a collection of subgroups, or as an assortment of individuals.

*Make your notes below. Specific quotes of significant speeches are helpful.*

Figure 9

committee work was somewhat slow and fumbling at the beginning. Students had mixed feelings about their ability to work well together, though most saw the activity as an interesting one.

The teacher sensed that the students who contributed least to the committee work were the same students who withheld participation in general class. He realized that group work was difficult because students had never been taught to evaluate and improve their operations. Since the use of committees, while not an unqualified success, had improved the number and the depth of student questions, he felt that it should be tried again. This time, however, he decided to include two sessions of diagnostic skill training.

To begin with, he (1) wrote a situation that had direct meaning for his class, (2) developed role instructions for the role players, (3) wrote guidelines for observers, and (4) jotted down a few discussion questions. They looked like this:

### Situation Statement

You are a classroom committee formed to plan the presentation of a mathematical concept to the rest of the class. The teacher has assigned you the idea that in a right triangle the sum of the squares of the sides are equal to the square of the hypotenuse.

This is your first meeting as a group. You will have about twenty minutes to make a tentative decision as to how you will handle the assignment and who will do what.

### Role-Player Instructions

(Note: Since the number of students in this hypothetical class is twenty-eight, two groups of fourteen can be formed, and half of each group will be role players while the other half will observe. This means that seven separate roles are needed. Role instructions should be designed so that problems common to such groups will occur. The role playing is really a way of illustrating problems so that they may be analyzed and discussed. Name of role players should be different from any names in the class.)

*John:*   You are used to leading groups, and you are a bit impatient with the time other students take to make decisions. You have the procedure all planned out, and you can save time by just telling the group about it and telling the other members what to do. If anyone has a different idea or calls for a chairman, you should express a great deal of impatience. Why waste time? If the group doesn't accept your idea, it will just talk and get nowhere. Push for the acceptance of your idea, and withdraw into silence if you are blocked. You'll show them!

*Howard:*   You resent John because he always pushes his ideas on the group and will not listen to anyone else. You don't mind hearing his ideas, but you want to see everyone's ideas expressed so that the group can make a choice. If John starts off by pushing people around, you will move to block him by asking that everyone contribute an idea. Don't let him be the boss. Try to include everyone.

*Mary:*   You like Howard and will move to support any ideas he presents. Say things like, "Howard's idea makes a lot of sense. Why don't we try it?" If you make a really good impression on Howard, maybe he will invite you to the dance.

*Rose:*   You are as impatient as John to get something done, but you agree with Howard that more people ought to be heard. You wish they would stop fighting because it makes it impossible for the group to get anywhere. Let them go at it for awhile and then say something like, "We're not getting anywhere. I wish we could just make a decision." If Mary says anything, ask her what her suggestion is. If anyone suggests having a chairman, throw up your hands and say, "We're wasting time. We don't need a chairman. We need to get to work."

*Jane:*   You are not sure just what to do, and you are afraid to say the wrong thing. Therefore, you remain silent unless someone asks you a direct question. If someone does, try to indicate that you agree with everyone, but do not say very much. If anyone complains about your silence, tell him that it is your business and to leave you alone.

*Peter:*   You want the committee to work. While you know that Howard and John will probably fight, you feel that you can make peace. When people begin to argue, you point out that they both have good ideas and that some compromise should be worked out. Another important contribution you make is that of summarizing. After every-

one has had a chance to speak, you will list all the points
they have made and ask, "Have I left anything out?"

*Frank:*    You want to be the leader of the group, and you see the
appointment of a chairman as the way to do it. Therefore, you will push for the election of a chairman, men-
tioning that you yourself have been a chairman of a
group before. Agree that everyone has a good idea, but
that the whole discussion will be a mess unless there is a
chairman to keep order. If John, who is usually talkative,
grows silent, you will point out that with John and Jane
not saying anything, the group can't really function.

The teacher should instruct role players to read role instructions over until they get all the ideas clear. They should play
the roles to the hilt, but should avoid overplaying them. If the
players do not seem to be playing the roles correctly, the teacher
may stop the proceedings and have them reread the instructions.

*Observer Guidelines*

In each subgroup of fourteen there will be seven role players and
seven observers. When the role play ends, each observer will report
his observations of the player to whom he was assigned. To help him
with this task, the teacher will prepare a sheet that will suggest what
it is he is looking for and on which he can make notes. Such a sheet
is illustrated in Figure 10.

The teacher may wish to have one or two students make
general observations of the group. This is particularly necessary
if there are more than twenty-eight students. When this is the
case, he may use the instructions in Figure 11.

Following the role playing and the reports by the observers,
the teacher will want to lead a discussion and analysis of what
has occurred. In order to channel the contributions of the students, he may wish to prepare a set of questions. Figure 12
illustrates.

Having developed these materials, the teacher is ready to
proceed with the exercise. This will be a Monday through Friday, or five-session affair. Orientation will take one session, role
playing two sessions, and group planning will take two sessions.
By the following Monday the groups should be ready to report.

*Guide for Observers*

As an observer, your task is to select a particular role player to observe, sit so that you face him or her, note your observations on this sheet, and be prepared to report your findings at the end of the role playing. (It is helpful if you take down actual words used.)

1. Comment on the concerns of your observee. Was he or she thinking of others in the group or merely focused on self?

2. Describe his or her actions. What effect did they seem to have on the others? Helpful? Hindering?

Figure 10

*General Observation Instructions*

Your task is to observe the group as a whole in order to determine what the leadership situation is, whether everyone is participating, and what is helping or blocking the group.

1.  Is the leadership in the hands of one or two people or is it shared by the group?

2.  Who speaks to whom? Does everyone participate?

3.  What is the atmosphere in the group? Tense? Comfortable? Silly?

Figure 11

*Discussion Questions*

The exercise in which you have just participated raises certain questions about how groups function. Your responses in writing to the following questions will be helpful in our discussion. (Use back of sheet if necessary.)

1. How do the hidden feelings of members affect the work of a committee?

2. How can a group involve *all* its members?

3. How could the functioning of the role-playing group have been improved?

Figure 12

To begin, the class is divided into four committees of equal size: A, B, C, and D. For the two days of the role playing, groups A and B will be together and groups C and D will be joined. For Thursday and Friday, each group will operate as a separate committee. The procedure is as follows:

*Five-Day Exercise*

1. FIRST SESSION: *Monday.* Teacher has chosen a mathematical concept to be taught to his class. He has analyzed it into four operations that have to be understood to grasp the main concept. He has prepared written assignments for each operation keyed to the text plus supplemental readings in the library.

2. Teacher brings to class seven copies of each of the four operation assignments, twenty-eight sheets in all, one for each student.

3. At the beginning of the class, he creates four committees of seven students each (A—B—C—D), and hands out the written assignments. While they read them, he answers questions and clarifies what is to be done.

4. Each student, as an individual, is to do the assignment at home, using the library as necessary. Assignments are to be completed by Thursday.

5   After twenty minutes clarifying the assignment, the teacher reminds the members of the class of their decision to try committee work again and announces that the next two days in class will be spent in what should be an interesting activity. It will consist of half the class working out a typical committee meeting while the rest observe and comment.

6. The teacher then informs the class that two of the committees (A and B) will form one group for the exercise and that the other two (C and D) will form a second group. Each group will then number fourteen.

7. In order to save time during the next session, the class will run through the exercise now.

8. Group A-B will meet at one end of the room while group C-D meets at the other. Their first task is to form seven pairs in each group.

9. One of each pair will be a role player; the other member of the pair will be his observer.

10. Teacher hands out one written role to each role player. (This means that the teacher needs to have two copies of each role.)

11. Role players are instructed: (1) not to let the others read the role; (2) to read the roles carefully; (3) to imagine how they would play these roles; and (4) to reread the roles to see if they have missed anything.

12. While the role players study their roles, the teacher gives out observer sheets to the remainder of the students. He explains that the students are to observe the process rather than the content of the role players' interactions.

13. Teacher then calls both groups together and explains that the role players will sit in an inner circle with their observers facing them. The seating would be as follows:

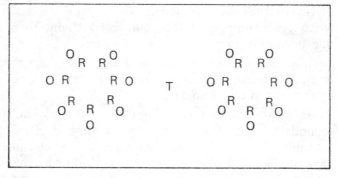

R—role players; O—observers; T—teacher

14. Teacher has each group seat themselves in the concentric circles so that they will know how to do it. They will take these seats immediately upon entering the class at the next session.

15. He then collects the role-playing instructions and the observer guide sheets so that they can be handed out at the beginning of the next session.

16. SECOND SESSION: *Tuesday*. Students enter and seat themselves in the two sets of concentric circles.

17. Teacher hands out sheets. In addition, he hands out tags with role names written large with magic marker on filing cards or oak tag. This will focus observers on the roles rather than on the actual students.

18. Teacher directs role players to read through their instructions and checks to see whether each role player has an observer. (In case of absence, he will have to make changes.)

19. Teacher reads the situation to both groups and reads it again. He answers clarifying questions and then directs role players to begin.

20. Role players begin their interaction, and the teacher keeps time. After about twenty minutes he breaks in (role players do not have to have finished) and directs observers to report their observations. Directly following each oral report, the role player reads his written instructions so that group can see how close the observer came.

21. Following this, the teacher leads a full class discussion on the question sheets, which are handed out at this time. There will be time only for a brief discussion, but the students will take the sheets home to be filled out and returned at the next session of the class.

22. Teacher announces that during the next session today's observers will become the role players and today's role players will become observers. The new role players will drop the instructions and play themselves in the same situation to see whether they can improve the group interaction.

23. THIRD SESSION: *Wednesday*. The two groups reconvene with reversed roles. The teacher again reads the situation and tells the groups to begin. (Fresh observer sheets are needed for this session.)

24. Teacher allows groups to run about twenty minutes or until they reach a decision. Then he stops them.

25. This time, each group will form a fourteen-member circle to discuss their observations and feelings for ten minutes.

26. For the remainder of the period, the entire class will discuss the exercise in terms of the homework questions and the discussions they have just finished.

27. At the end of the session, the teacher announces that the exercise is over and that the committees will begin their work tomorrow, having a chance to put new understandings and learnings to the test in an actual situation.
28. FOURTH SESSION: *Thursday.* The four committees meet to begin their planning. They will spend the last ten minutes of the period discussing their process.
29. FIFTH SESSION: *Friday.* Groups will finish their planning, decide on which days they will report to the class, and again check their process during the last ten minutes.

This exercise should provide the class with an interesting experience and should measurably improve each group's performance. (See Chapter 5 for evaluation procedures.)

In addition to the specific committee work, the awareness of the process level of communication can have far-reaching effects on participation in the class if the exercise is followed up. Such follow-up might include setting aside fifteen minutes each week to ask, "How are we doing?" In these sessions, the teacher should also participate, talking about how he feels toward the class. Does he feel that students are participating? Are they taking any responsibility for their own learning? Are they raising any really thoughtful questions about the subject matter? Are they supplying maintenance functions in class discussion in order to help their fellow classmates feel more free to participate?

Since the enhancement of communication flow and the development of an uninhibited atmosphere for learning needs to be nurtured through teacher and student interactions, two points should be underlined. First, participation can be a much more meaningful activity than it is in many classrooms. Participation is not mere talk or response to a recitation method where the teacher asks questions and individual students answer with little awareness of each other. It is interesting to see a student whose raised hand has been recognized by the teacher begin to answer the question. If he becomes unsure of his response or falters at any moment, ten other hands shoot up instantly with no discernible consideration for his feelings.

At the same time, many hands are *not* raised, and one wonders what is going on in the owners' minds. The end result is that students do not really explore ideas or help each other to understand the subject matter more fully. Yet, with many hands in the air, many teachers are pleased at the "participation" in the class. What is suggested in the notion of interaction analysis is that this student eagerness is only a first step and needs much further development.

The second point to be underlined is that the exercises in this book are meant as beginnings. After a month or two of being together, awareness and skills in both content and process levels ought to become internalized so that there is less need for crutches. But the crutches *are* necessary in the beginning if teacher and students are to break through the overformality that makes the classroom more a game than a vital and meaningful part of living.

## Building the Group

In order to move toward group status, any aggregate of people must find a mutually satisfactory way of meeting two kinds of needs. They must feel a sense of progress toward goals (*task functions*), and they must develop a supportive atmosphere (*maintenance functions*). Needs for progress begin to be met when members internalize goals—when they begin to relate them to their own personal framework of understanding, put them in their own language, and see them as personally valuable. This is best done by having members participate in the formulation of goals.

Needs for a supportive atmosphere begin to be met when members recognize the contributions of others, call them by name, and indicate that they have heard what others have said. Without such a supportive atmosphere, only a few strong members speak out, and even they tend to seek a dependency relationship with the appointed leader (in this case, the teacher).

Goal progress rests on internalization, and atmosphere progress rests on interpersonal knowledge and respect. This latter condition is commonly called "getting to know each other."

Work on both these areas should begin early in the life span of any classroom group, and since progress is difficult, this work should be reinforced as the year unfolds. Many avenues toward progress exist, and the inventive teacher will undoubtedly develop his own methods. One approach that seems workable on many age levels is the following:

### Background Sharing Exercise

*Situation:* This is a class in (*fill in grade level and subject*). It is the first week of the school year. Students know some of their fellows, but not all. Each has had some experiences in the subject during the preceding year(s) and/or expectations concerning this year's work. Each, also, has a wealth of hobbies, interests, experiences, and aspirations, which have developed during the years in which he has lived. In addition, he has probably come to believe that most of this background is not relevant to normal classroom behavior. He probably sees communication with his peers in the classroom mostly in terms of misbehavior, and feels quite inadequate in setting his own goals for learning. After all, that is the teacher's job.

*Intent:* The teacher realizes the norms of dependency and inter-student competition that have been developed by many teachers. He also accepts his own position as subject-matter expert. There certainly *are* valid reasons why *he* is the teacher and *they* are the students. However, he feels that student internalization of learning goals plus the creation of a mutually supportive atmosphere are vital ingredients in effective teaching and learning. His initial intent is to aid his class in reevaluating and changing the classroom norms they have come to expect. Feeling that a lecture on this subject would be less effective than a shared experience, he structures the first few sessions of the class in such a way that students are active from the beginning.

*General Conditions:*
1. Norm changing is a delicate and difficult process. Teacher cannot expect immediate success. Patience and faith are needed.
2. Natural fears of "wasting time" and "failing to cover the ground" will occur to both teacher and students, since they are not accustomed to this new way of learning. Justification must come from the fact that the teacher *is* dealing directly with the

subject matter, that he is involved in teaching study skills, and that he is motivating the class.

3. It is important that the teacher explain the exercise and why he thinks it is important. He should enlist his students' feeling of adventure. A feeling of "Let's explore together" is a vital prerequisite.

4. As the exercise proceeds, the students will probably be wondering whether the teacher is really sincere. Does he really want them to get to know each other? Does he really value what *they* think about the course? After all, they've been fooled before.

5. Students will need help in learning how to go about expressing their ideas and developing them into proposals for learning. (Even the teacher could sharpen his own skills in this area.)

Goals: Teacher purposes for this exercise may be expressed as follows: As a result of this experience, students will:

1. Know each other's names.
2. Know something about each other in terms of hobbies, interests, and ambitions.
3. Feel freer to speak out in class.
4. Tend more to support each other.
5. Review previous learnings in this subject.
6. Develop and describe future learnings.
7. Define and list resources in terms of films, printed materials, the community, field trip opportunities, and human resources such as the librarian.
8. Suggest ways of learning this subject.
9. Suggest ways in which the specialized knowledge of the teacher can best be used.

*Procedures*

1. SESSION ONE: Teacher asks class whether all students know each other. If there are some who do not, the teacher suggests that since they will spend a school year together, it would probably help to get acquainted. Next, he asks

what they know about the subject and what they expect to learn this year.

2. (Since a beginning class is an aggregate, and since the question of expectations is a difficult one, it may be expected that a few students will struggle with it while the rest remain silent.)

3. After five-minutes discussion, the teacher says that he has a number of ideas himself, but that he would like to know what they think first. He realizes that this is not an easy assignment, and would they like to try an experiment.

4. The student response will probably be a tentative "yes" subject to hearing more about the teacher's idea.

5. Teacher explains that what he has in mind should help students to know each other better and develop their problem-solving abilities. Both of these will be important to the work of the class in future.

6. The exercise will consist of meeting in pairs for five minutes, combining pairs into quartets for five minutes, combining quartets into octets for ten minutes, and writing the results of octet discussions for five minutes.

7. Each subgrouping will have two tasks: (1) to share names, hobbies, and interests; (2) to determine two or three things that they especially want to learn in this course.

8. To begin the procedure, the teacher assigns each student a number in random fashion (e.g., in a class of thirty-two students, 1, 2, 3, . . . 32).

*Organization of Sessions*

SESSION ONE:

Orientation (Procedures 1-8)                                    15 minutes

Pairs meet

| 1 | 2 | 3 | 4 | 5 | 6 | 7 | 8 |
|---|---|---|---|---|---|---|---|
| 9 | 10 | 11 | 12 | 13 | 14 | 15 | 16 |
| 17 | 18 | 19 | 20 | 21 | 22 | 23 | 24 |
| 25 | 26 | 27 | 28 | 29 | 30 | 31 | 32 |

5 minutes

Quartets meet:

| 1 | 2 | 3 | 4 | 5 | 6 | 7 | 8 |
|---|---|---|---|---|---|---|---|
| 9 | 10 | 11 | 12 | 13 | 14 | 15 | 16 |
| 17 | 18 | 19 | 20 | 21 | 22 | 23 | 24 |
| 25 | 26 | 27 | 28 | 29 | 30 | 31 | 32 |

5 minutes

Octets meet:

| 1 | 2 | 3 | 4 | 5 | 6 | 7 | 8 | |
|---|---|---|---|---|---|---|---|---|
| 9 | 10 | 11 | 12 | 13 | 14 | 15 | 16 | |
| 17 | 18 | 19 | 20 | 21 | 22 | 23 | 24 | |
| 25 | 26 | 27 | 28 | 29 | 30 | 31 | 32 | 10 minutes |

Octets will appoint a secretary to record with ball-point pen on ditto master those things students have said they want to learn.                                          5 minutes

SESSION TWO:

Teacher has run off copies of yesterday's lists so that each student receives four sheets—one from each octet.

For the first five minutes, each student reads through the lists and makes notes as further ideas occur to him.

Format for the second session begins with the same pairs as first session, but changes the membership of the quartets and octets so that more face-to-face relationships develop. The assignment is the same: #7 of page 126.

Individual student reading and note-making.                          5 minutes

Pairs meet:

| 1 | 2 | 9 | 10 | 17 | 18 | 25 | 26 | |
|---|---|---|----|----|----|----|----|---|
| 3 | 4 | 11 | 12 | 19 | 20 | 27 | 28 | |
| 5 | 6 | 13 | 14 | 21 | 22 | 29 | 30 | |
| 7 | 8 | 15 | 16 | 23 | 24 | 31 | 32 | 5 minutes |

Quartets:

| 1 | 2 | 9 | 10 | 17 | 18 | 25 | 26 | |
|---|---|---|----|----|----|----|----|---|
| 3 | 4 | 11 | 12 | 19 | 20 | 27 | 28 | |
| 5 | 6 | 13 | 14 | 21 | 22 | 29 | 30 | |
| 7 | 8 | 15 | 16 | 23 | 24 | 31 | 32 | 5 minutes |

Octets:

| 1 | 2 | 9 | 10 | 17 | 18 | 25 | 26 | |
|---|---|---|----|----|----|----|----|---|
| 3 | 4 | 11 | 12 | 19 | 20 | 27 | 28 | |
| 5 | 6 | 13 | 14 | 21 | 22 | 29 | 30 | |
| 7 | 8 | 15 | 16 | 23 | 24 | 31 | 32 | 10 minutes |

Writing of revisions and additions from each octet on paper to be handed to teacher.                          10 minutes

SESSION THREE:

Teacher reviews student writing from session two and organizes items under main headings. Copies are duplicated for students.

For the first five minutes, each student will read and make notes and additions on his sheet as in session two.

For the remainder of the session, the teacher will plan with the class what is to be taught first, how it can be handled in terms of method, what resources are available and how they can be used, and what method of evaluation will be best.

During this session, the teacher's most valuable contribution can be suggestions in terms of methods. Lectures, demonstrations, discussions, projects, panels, committees, use of textbook, written and visual materials, field trips, guest speakers, and the like may be suggested where they seem appropriate. It may be helpful to invite resource people from the staff to come in for half the period to help in the planning (e.g., librarian, audiovisual director, curriculum director, school nurse or doctor, school psychologist).

At this session, ideas of what objectives will be set, what teacher and students will do, when they will do what, and how they will evaluate —all these should be listed on the chalkboard.

The task of organizing these ideas into a flow chart for a month's work (or whatever time period seems appropriate) will not be accomplished during this period—it will have to wait for session four.

SESSION FOUR:

The exercise thus far should do much to make the group more cohesive, but full participation will take much more time. At this point, the subgroups have met to share ideas, but they have not had the more difficult task of decision making.

During session four, therefore, their assignment is to map out the activities for the next two to three or four weeks based on the points of discussion in session three.

As they move from group to larger group, they will have to make decisions by choosing from alternative plans or combining and modifying proposals.

In session four, they will begin with octets, move to sixteens, and finish as the full class.

Teacher should remind them that the norm of introductions and use of each other's names still applies. Teacher should sit in on some of the groups and reinforce maintenance functions.

Teacher reviews ideas of session three and assigns groups
the task of deciding what will be done, when, and by
whom.                                                    10 minutes

Octets:

| 1 | 2 | 11 | 12 | 21 | 22 | 31 | 32 |
|---|---|----|----|----|----|----|----|
| 7 | 8 | 13 | 14 | 19 | 20 | 25 | 26 |
| 3 | 4 | 29 | 30 | 9  | 10 | 23 | 24 |
| 5 | 6 | 27 | 28 | 15 | 16 | 17 | 18 |

10 minutes

Sixteens:

| 1 | 2 | 11 | 12 | 21 | 22 | 31 | 32 |
|---|---|----|----|----|----|----|----|
| 7 | 8 | 13 | 14 | 19 | 20 | 25 | 26 |
| 3 | 4 | 29 | 30 | 9  | 10 | 23 | 24 |
| 5 | 6 | 27 | 28 | 15 | 16 | 17 | 18 |

10 minutes

Total Class: Final decision as to what will be done, when, and by whom. One student may record decision on the chalkboard, using a checkerboard grid to indicate sessions.        15 minutes

SESSION FIVE:

This session, under teacher direction, may be used to tie up any loose ends. At the close of the period, everyone should know what is going to happen during the next few weeks and what part they and the teacher will play.

An important item for this session is a discussion of how well students think they got to know each other, and how they feel about this.

Though it is unlikely that the students will do anything like a perfect job of planning, the exercise should be a giant step toward learning how to plan for learning. The teacher may wish to hand out and collect a short reaction sheet at the end of session four. These data can spark the discussion of "How did we do?" during session five.

## Listening Skill Session

Thus far, the exercises have involved interacting groups of various sizes. Tasks have ranged from getting to know each other to sharpening group awareness of the process level of communication. From time to time, however, the teacher and/or the students may identify specific skills that need to be developed. One such specific skill is listening.

The idea of developing skill in listening seems, at first glance, to be an absurd one. People spend a good deal of their waking moments listening. Why should they have to develop a skill they already have? Perhaps a skill exercise in this area is necessary because listening is too often taken for granted. Actually, most groups that begin to look at their process as well as their content identify listening as a skill that needs improving.

It takes only a little thought to verify this statement. How many times do we have the experience of not really understanding what is being said? How many times are our messages misunderstood or only partly understood? Are we sometimes so concerned with what *we* are planning to say that we only partially listen to the other person? And when the listening is imperfect, how do we find out about it? Do we ask to have it repeated? If we repeated, in our words, what another has said, would he recognize it as his message? Is the act of listening really as simple as we think it is?

As it is used in this book, the concept of interaction would suggest a mutual responsibility of speaker and hearer in the listening process. Rather than the term *listening*, then, it might be more accurate to think in terms of skill in concentration and mutual clarification.

In the following skill session, listening is examined behaviorally as a vital factor in the improvement of group communication.

*Procedure*

1. Teacher distributes (or writes on the chalkboard) three or four discussion topics that he has composed out of his knowledge of the interests and backgrounds of his students.
2. He then divides the class into groups of three students seated as far apart as space permits.
3. He explains that each group must select one of the discussion topics. Give two or three minutes for this.
4. The trios are to discuss the topic they have chosen. Discussion is unstructured except that each person who speaks (except the first, of course) must paraphrase what the last person has said before he himself speaks. This paraphrasing must be done to satisfaction of the last speaker.
5. Teacher allows discussions to continue for fifteen to twenty minutes. He then stops them and has them discuss the exercise for a few minutes still in the trios.
6. The short discussion is followed by a general class discussion concerning the experience. The following questions may be used as guidelines:

How difficult was it to paraphrase?
Did the difficulty depend on the clarity of the speaker?

Did it depend on how long he spoke or how many ideas he tried
    to get across at a time?

Did you find that *your* listeners had trouble with your messages?

Do you usually listen this intently?

Is it sometimes hard to follow ideas in class?

How can we improve our communication?

## Nondirective Discussion Leadership

Teacher direction is an essential part of each of the exercises
detailed above. In explaining and motivating the group work and
in the short talks at the end, the teacher's understanding of
group process and skill in discussion leadership is a vital ingredient. As such, it should be considered separately.

It has been noted in Chapter 2 that the common pattern of
classroom interaction is from the teacher to John, back to the
teacher, to Mary, back to the teacher, to Fred, back to the
teacher, and so on. This pattern may be most appropriate when
the class is engaged in asking specific questions of the teacher;
for the purposes of a discussion, however, it is most inappropriate. Good discussion leadership acts to bring out maximum
participation and to extend the communications pattern so that
student speaks to student without having to plug into the
teacher switchboard.

Because students have learned through their schooling years
to see the teacher as a switchboard, and because so many teachers play this role, a change in pattern will come about only
through a change in teacher behavior. Such change should move
from directive, dominating, dependency creating leadership
toward nondirective, member freeing leadership.[1] In perform-
ing such a function (or set of functions), the teacher should
seek to move out of his usual bottleneck position in the discussion while at the same time acting to reinforce students'

[1] Thomas Gordon, *Group-Centered Leadership: A Way for Releasing the
Creative Power of Groups* (Boston: Houghton Mifflin Co., 1955). While
the whole book is extremely valuable, Chapter 8, "A Description of the
Group-Centered Leader," is especially relevant. See also Carl R. Rogers,
*Client-Centered Therapy*, Chapter 9, "Student-Centered Teaching" (Bos-
ton: Houghton Mifflin Co., 1965).

confidence in their own ability. Since they tend to have limited self-confidence, they may be expected to make it difficult, at least initially, for the teacher to move. When the teacher begins to change the ways in which he plays his role, he begins to make it necessary for students to change behaviors that they are used to. Yet such change is possible, and it need not be painful. The results of the change are well worth the trouble since there are few feelings as good as that of feeling competent in self-direction. Such an aim is what all schools say they strive for; nondirective discussion leadership is merely a first step in that direction.

Before proceeding further, it might be well to define the term and specify teacher behavior. *Nondirective teaching* might perhaps better be called non-manipulating or non-suffocating teaching. It consists of teacher behavior designed to cut through the dependency needs of students by refusing to do their thinking and structuring for them. This does not mean, in any sense, that direction of some sort is not necessary; rather, it means that the teacher sees his role as fostering self-direction on the part of the students. This is not an easy process in the beginning for either teacher or students because of the preponderance of traditional practice that puts the teacher in the driver's seat and tends to glue him there through his own expression of ego need to be the giver of all knowledge and through the students' acceptance of a comfortable passive role. Speaking of the preparation of teachers to change their highly directive roles, Sarason and his colleagues have said:

> . . . in describing our experiences we emphasize not the amount of time, but what we consider to be a way of structuring the relationship between students and instructors, which is different from more conventional procedures. Briefly, and to recapitulate: The students were rarely *given* ideas of starting points; they had to subject their ideas, opinions, and suggestions to discussion; they were more or less forced to learn to give expression to and to depend upon *their* curiosity; they could express their puzzlements and ignorance without viewing them as signs of stupidity but as aids to productive learning; and they were enabled to see for themselves the complexity and selectivity of their own observational processes and their effects on action. To accomplish these things, it is far from sufficient to say to students: "Be curious. Use your own ideas. Do not be afraid to be wrong! etc." Unless students actually begin to respond in these

ways and in so doing experience an awareness of a change in their thinking and perspective, verbal suggestions are not likely to be effective. It is essential to our approach to expect that students will and must struggle, because learning to think independently and to utilize one's own intellectual resources is never easy, particularly when previous learning has been of the passive dependent variety.[2]

If such a nondirective stance is important, it certainly should begin with the teacher in his own training. That such teacher behavior is *not* characteristic of today's teachers is borne out in the results of an increasing number of studies that document through stenographic reports, tape recordings, and kinescopes what *is* going on in American classrooms. Typical of such studies is Bellack's, which reports that:

> Teachers dominate the verbal activities of the classrooms studied. The teacher-pupil ratio of activity in terms of lines spoken is approximately 3 to 1; in terms of moves, the ratio is about 3 to 2. Therefore, regardless of the unit considered, teachers are considerably more active than pupils in amount of verbal activity.[3]

Nondirectiveness on the part of the teacher stems from his understanding of the effects of various styles of leader behavior. Teachers, traditionally, are concerned with promoting student participation in the class. They tend to mention the participation rate often and frequently base part of a student's grade on his overt involvement in class discussion. Yet, as Gordon points out:

> The more dependent the group is upon its leader, the more his contribution will inhibit the participation of other members. The greater the status or prestige differential is between the leader and the members (as perceived by the members), the more likely the leader's contributions will inhibit participation of the members.[4]

In response to such data, the teacher who feels that increasing student self-direction leads to worthwhile learning

[2] Seymour B. Sarason, Kenneth Davidson, and Burton Blatt, *The Preparation of Teachers* (New York: John Wiley and Sons, Inc., 1962), pp. 90-91. Used by permission.
[3] Arno A. Bellack, *Theory and Research in Teaching* (New York: Bureau of Publications, Teachers College, Columbia University, 1963), p. 110.
[4] Gordon, *Group-Centered Leadership*, p. 250.

experiences may wish to modify the role he now plays as discussion leader. If so, he will want to try out some new leader behaviors.

Such new behaviors emphasize restructuring the usual communication network, which makes him willingly or unwillingly a bottleneck that serves to block free student-to-student interaction. In seeking to accomplish this modification, he will realize that student behavior will also have to change and that this will not happen immediately. In effect, he is attempting to teach his students skills in interaction.

1.  Teacher begins with the recognition that the traditional seating arrangement in rows was developed for efficiency in one-way transmission of information.
2.  If he wishes to encourage students to speak to students, he will have to seat them in a circle or semicircle.
3.  Since knowledge of a subject is prerequisite to its discussion, the topic should be one that has been experienced by the students either directly or through instructional materials.
4.  Some class discussions will center on subject matter, some on methodology, some on evaluation of what has been done.
5.  Motivation will probably center on the degree of feeling that participants bring to the subject matter of a discussion. If few care one way or the other, no method or gimmick of any sort will be successful in involving the students.
6.  The teacher may begin by stating (or restating) the problem, though as the group begins to mature, this role can be taken by a student.
7.  As students begin to express feelings and opinions or to ask questions, it should be expected initially that these will be addressed to the teacher as judge, final arbiter, and fount of all really worthwhile knowledge and opinion.
8.  It is the teacher's job at this junction to clarify and reflect on what has been said, but avoiding a bottlenecking role even when students attempt to place him within it.
9.  In the playing of a nondirective role, the teacher will:
    a.  Listen and communicate to the class that he is aware of and interested in what is being said.
    b.  Accept and respect students' ideas while helping them clarify their thoughts.
    c.  Reflect ideas by rephrasing them to be sure that full meaning is communicated.
    d.  Reflect feelings by raising questions when he senses responses are not being stated directly.
    e.  Help students to elaborate their own and others' ideas.

f.   Connect ideas and build concepts from what students are saying.
g.   Raise questions about need for summarizing, but avoid taking the role himself.
h.   Raise process analysis questions, but allow the group freedom to act upon or ignore his comments.

It can be seen from the description in number 9 above that the nondirective discussion leader is most active. The main differences between this behavior and that usually displayed by teachers are that he (1) restricts the number of words he uses in order to provide opportunity for more student participation, (2) listens intently and gives evidence that he is listening, (3) avoids judgmental comments, throwing the decision making out to the class, (4) shows acceptance of student contribution (this does not mean mere agreement with everything since he is not being the judge), and (5) acts as a model of helpful task and maintenance functions for the group so that students may use these behaviors themselves. Such teacher behavior, of course, requires practice, but the very act of practicing can be an exciting, fulfilling one as the aggregate begins to become a participating group.

Two things need to be underlined at this point. First, the movement of a class from an aggregate to a group is a slow, developmental process. Students are learning communication skills, and this takes time. The teacher who expects an instant change will be disappointed, and disappointment may lead him to fall back on more familiar dominating behavior. If he has patience, however, it will not take the class long to react. Their unspoken question will be, "Do you really mean this behavior, or are you suddenly going to pull the rug out from under us?"

Second, the teacher needs to enlarge his concept of class participation.[5] In the past this has meant the student's saying almost anything, particularly asking the teacher a question to prove he has studied the material and is interested or replying to a direct question from the teacher. In the framework of this book, student participation includes the skillful application of task or maintenance functions when they are needed to help the group solve its problem or make a decision or evaluate what has gone on. In this sense, the teacher's task becomes more complex. He must help to create a supportive environment that

[5] See comments regarding student participation, pp. 122-123 of this book.

will bring students out, *and* he must also help them to sharpen their communications skills so that they become less dependent on his spoon-feeding.

The following dialogue is illustrative of the beginning of a class discussion conducted by a nondirective teacher.

| | | |
|---|---|---|
| 1. | *Teacher:* | For the past week we have been exploring the England of Elizabeth the First. Since it seems hard to discuss anything looking at the backs of people's heads I have moved the desks into a circle. I think we agreed yesterday that we wanted to discuss the development leading to England's emergence as a world power. Shall we begin? |
| 2. | *Sandra:* | *After a fifteen-second silence.* It feels sort of funny to sit in a circle. |
| 3. | *Teacher:* | *Smiles.* |
| 4. | *Frank:* | The class looks different. |
| 5. | *Teacher:* | *Smiles and nods agreement.* |
| 6. | *Howard:* | I don't think I've seen some of these people face to face. |
| 7. | *Teacher:* | *After more silence.* I am thinking that I agree with Frank. The class does look a little different, but at least *I* usually see everyone's face. I'm wondering how others feel. |

| | | |
|---|---|---|
| 1. | | The teacher sets the scene, commenting on the new physical arrangement and reminding class of the discussion question. |
| 3 and 5. | | Teacher accepts comments, but does not respond, giving other students a chance to comment. |
| 7. | | Teacher moves from silence to verbal support of expression of feelings and throws leadership back to group. |

| | | |
|---|---|---|
| 8. | *Susan:* | I like it. |
| 9. | *Mike:* | It's like Thanksgiving with everyone sitting around the table. |
| 10. | *Fred:* | Boy, you must have a big family. |
| 11. | *Mike:* | Well, not quite this big. |
| 12. | *Harry:* | Maybe we ought to get a turkey. |
| 13. | *Lee:* | Let's wait until we get to the Pilgrims. |
| 14. | *Class laughs and teacher joins in.* | |
| 15. | *Mike:* | Yeah. We're supposed to be having a discussion. |
| 16. | *Howard:* | All right, Mike, go ahead and discuss. |
| 17. | *Susan:* | *To teacher.* How should we go about it, Mr. Harris? |

18. *Teacher:*   Well, I guess there are a number of ways to begin, but I'm wondering if we are leaving Mike and Howard hanging.
19. *Mike:*   Oh that's all right. Go ahead.
20. *Howard:*   It's not all right with me. How come you cut me off, Susan?
21. *Susan:*   I really hadn't thought about it. Sorry.
22. *Teacher:*   It's interesting to me the way groups make decisions. We were talking about how it felt to sit in a circle. Did we need to decide to leave that subject before going on?
23. *Fred:*   It was Harry's turkey.
24. *Harry:*   And then Joe said wait for the Pilgrims.
25. *Jeanette:*   And here we are.
26. *Mary:*   What do we do now?

---

13.   Joe's remark served to break the slight tension and to bring the conversation back to the discussion topic.

15 and 16.   Mike and Howard picked up on Joe's remark.

17.   Susan followed their lead, but threw the lead to teacher.

18.   Teacher accepted comment, but made a process comment about whether Mike and Howard had been bypassed.

22.   Teacher generalized his earlier process comment to question the decision-making process.

26.   Mary asks for direction, and teacher resists urge to tell her.

---

27. *Jack:*   I'd like to say something about this circle thing.
28. *Harry:*   Go ahead.
29. *Jack:*   I think it makes it easier to talk.
30. *Howard:*   I hope you don't stop.
31. *Jack:*   Maybe I won't.
32. *Mary:*   Should we talk about the topic?
33. *Mike:*   *Humorously.* We have to make a group decision.
34. *Class laughs.*
35. *Howard:*   Let's agree that anybody can say what they're feeling even if it isn't on the topic.
36. *Mary:*   But that would be confusing.
37. *Mike:*   What do you think, Mr. Harris?
38. *Teacher:*   I think it's an interesting idea, though Mary might be right. We need everyone's help in deciding.
39. *Mary:*   You're not going to tell us the answer?
40. *Teacher:*   I'm not sure I know the answer, Mary. Perhaps

we should know more about what Howard had in mind.

41.  *Harry:*    What did you have in mind, Howie?

42.  *Howard:*   I just thought we could decide to leave the talk about sitting in a circle, which I'm getting tired of anyway, if we could feel free to return to it like Jack if a thought hit us.

43.  *Fred:*     That sounds all right to me.

---

27.  Jack makes comment on circle. From student response, it appears that he is usually silent. They reinforce him (28 and 30).

32.  Mary again asks for direction.

33.  Mike makes it a joke, but *does* ask for group decision.

35.  Howard asks for a group norm.

36.  Mary questions it.

37.  Mike throws it back to teacher.

38.  Teacher asks group.

39.  Mary wants clarification.

40.  Teacher does not refuse, but helps group to elaborate Howard's idea.

42-43.  Howard elaborates and Fred supports.

---

44.  *Mary:*     I still think it might get confusing, but if Mr. Harris doesn't know the answer, neither do I. I'd be willing to try it.

45.  *Jeanette:* Fine. Let's get on with it. Now, when the Spanish Armada sailed . . .

46.  *Mike:*     Jeanette.

47.  *Jeanette:* Yes?

48.  *Mike:*     Seriously, now. I don't want to cut you off, but I don't think the group really made this decision.

49.  *Jeanette:* Oh, for goodness sake!

50.  *Jack:*     I think he's right, Jeanette. If you start talking before you check the decision, how do you know that anyone's listening?

51.  *Jeanette:* Well, what do you want me to do?

52.  *Susan:*    What I should have done before. Ask everybody if they are ready to discuss the topic.

53.  *Jeanette:* Okay. (*To class.*) Are we ready to discuss the topic?

54.  *Mike:*     *Breaking several seconds of silence.* I'm ready.

55.  *Fred:*     So am I.

56.  *General murmur of assent with nodding heads.*

57.  *Jeanette:*    All right. Now, I think we should start with the
Armada. When Elizabeth began . . .

---

44-45.  Mary withdraws her objection and Jeanette begins discussion.
46-52.  Mike raises question about group decision and gets Jack's support. Susan shows that she has been thinking about her earlier effort to get discussion started.
53-55.  A group decision is made (as well as it can be in this beginning group) and Jeanette begins. (*Note:* Teacher has moved into the background, though he will want to check the feelings of students about this at a later time.)

---

## Agree-Disagree Exercise

Often teachers wish to know how students feel about the content of the course, how it is being taught, how it might be improved to meet their needs. Such information could be quite valuable to all concerned. While the aggregate is working its way toward group maturity, however, teachers may be reluctant to open up such questions for discussion. And even when they do, the chance of getting anything close to a full group response is quite small. Until a class develops trust that their ideas are really valued, and until students develop some skills in expressing ideas in a constructive way, communication of feelings is difficult. But the process has to begin somewhere, and one method that seems to offer promise is the agree-disagree exercise.

Simply put, this type of exercise consists of a set of written statements concerning a particular area of interest. The student, receiving a copy of the statements, reads them through and indicates his agreement or disagreement with each item.

If ten statements are composed so that five will favor one point of view and five favor another, it is a simple task to determine general attitudes. It is also easy to check student opinions individually and generally.

As is the case with all such data, the teacher may collect the papers for his own purposes. On the other hand, the students themselves may wish to analyze the findings in order to tap the otherwise unexpressed feelings of their peers. As the trust level grows in the class, it is usually wise for the teacher to have students collect, analyze, and report such data.

A more sophisticated use of the device involves an effort to reach consensus in the group. While anyone can, if instructed, indicate agreement *or* disagreement, it is safe to assume that students will have mixed feelings on a number of the items. Thus, the teacher may use the statements in the following way:

1. Announce that the sheets contain a number of statements about *X* (whatever the subject may be), and that each student is to read them carefully and mark them agree or disagree.

2. After allowing enough time for reading and reacting, divide the class into groups of five. These groups are to arrive at a consensus concerning their agreement or disagreement with each item. They may change the wording in any way that will help them make these decisions.

3. Each group then will report their conclusions to the rest of the class, including their changes in the wording of items and their reasons for making the changes.

4. The teacher may wish to have the entire class reach consensus, or he may end the exercise after the groups have reported and the class has had time to discuss the reports.

This procedure, whether the entire class reaches a consensus or not, brings out clearly the thinking of the students concerning the main issues raised. In addition, it creates a sense of sharing and communicating that will encourage total class participation. Its success will, of course, be enhanced to the degree that the teacher follows through in response to the opinions brought out. Such follow-through should include trying out some of the suggestions *and* allowing more time for expression of feelings at a later date. It would be true to the notion of group growth if the students themselves could conduct the second exercise. By the third or fourth time, the class usually outgrows the need for the exercise and begins to talk more freely.

A specimen of an agree-disagree exercise appears in Figure 13. Examination of the items will show a number of things. First, they are all concerned with questions of class procedure and teacher behavior. Second, they are divided between desires

*Agree-Disagree Exercise*

Read each of the items below carefully and indicate your agreement or disagreement by placing an X on the appropriate line to the left.

*Agree*  *Disagree*

1. The teacher ought to do all the planning in the course because he knows most about the subject matter.

_____  _____

2. Outside reading should always be handled by having each student turn in a written book report to the teacher.

_____  _____

3. Using student committees for learning and reporting is a valuable part of the course.

_____  _____

4. Lecturing by the teacher is the best way to cover the subject matter.

_____  _____

5. Teachers should allow the students to participate in planning the course work.

_____  _____

6. Students can often learn more from each other than they can from the teacher.

_____  _____

7. Seats should be moved into a circle for class discussions.

_____  _____

8. Committee work wastes too much time. The teacher should do the teaching.

_____  _____

9. It is important that students in a class know each other and have a chance to talk to each other while the class is in session.

_____  _____

10. The teacher should call on people in class when they do not volunteer.

_____  _____

Figure 13

for teacher direction and desires for student direction and freedom. Items 1, 2, 4, 8, and 10 call for teacher direction while items 3, 5, 6, 7, and 9 call for student direction. In addition, item 1 is the opposite of item 5 and item 3 is the opposite of item 8. The opposite items serve to check each other, but also they introduce alternatives for student thinking. Use of this exercise should provoke a great deal of controversy and discussion.


## Buzz Groups

It is easier to speak freely in small groups than it is in large ones. It is even easier in *very* small groups. A teacher's constant problem is the promotion of full participation in the class which is a very large small group (twenty-five to thirty seems average). In attempting to deal with this problem, he faces the inhibitions caused by his own behavior, the aggregate status of the class, and the difficulties students have in speaking freely before an audience that may not support or even listen very carefully to what they are saying.

Typical teacher behavior seems to ignore or be unaware of these participation blocks. Instead of waiting until a student makes a contribution and then reinforcing this, a teacher may attempt to draw in silent members by putting them on the spot with a direct question. Since the teacher himself, placed on the receiving end in one of his college classes, could probably do little more than give a quick unthoughtful answer, it is fairly safe to assume that the student will not respond to probing with any change in his usual silent behavior. (It is true that some people *do* need a direct question or comment from the leader to get started, but this procedure is a chancey one to experiment with in the class situation before the aggregate has become a group.)

Besides the obvious problem of embarrassing the student and increasing his silent withdrawal, the teacher's move of "pitchforking" students into discussion has a number of other drawbacks. For one thing, it involves rejecting the enthusiastically raised hands of the strong participators who may begin to fall by the wayside from neglect. For another, it reduces the *type* of participating to a series of short responses to teacher questions. Like most of the teacher's classroom behaviors, the recitation lesson stems from his basic concepts (or lack of clear concepts) of how people learn and of how groups interact.

An alternative to the "pitchforking" or "tooth pulling" approach to broader participation is the buzz group. A teacher who wishes to produce an atmosphere in which more students will contribute to a discussion may begin the session by dividing the class into groups of five to explore ideas for ten minutes. At the end of the allotted time, the class reconvenes for a general discussion. Since more people have had an opportunity to speak and to motivate themselves in the buzz session, the notion is that more individual students will contribute in the general discussion.

Buzz groups can be used at the beginning, middle, or end of a class session for a number of purposes. The two models below are illustrative:

*Beginning Discussion*

1. Either from his own feelings concerning the main points to be discussed, or from the decisions of the class at a previous session, the teacher prepares written guidelines for each participant.

2. At the previous session (to save time if it seems necessary) he explains that the class will begin with ten minutes of small-group discussion, and then selects the groups (or lets them select themselves). Each group will be not less than four nor more than six students. Following the ten minutes, the entire class will reconvene to carry on a general discussion, which the small groups have started.

3. (*Notes:* [a] It is not necessary for the buzz groups to come to any conclusions. This is merely a warm-up for the class discussion. [b] The written guidelines may be passed out a day ahead so that students will have time to think about the questions.)

4. On the day of the discussion, the teacher directs students to form the buzz groups and begin their discussions. (As the group matures, the students themselves can begin the process. A definite sign of an aggregate is the class that waits to be called to order each time it meets.)

5. Teacher acts as timekeeper and calls a halt to the buzz groups at the end of the ten minutes. (During this time, he

may wish to sit in on one or more of the groups. And, if he does this, he may wish at some future time to check the impact on students of his joining the group. In the beginning stages, his presence will probably inhibit some students.)

6.   After he has called time, the teacher will have the students move their chairs into a total class setting and begin the discussion.

7.   (*Notes:* [a] See the description of discussion leader behavior on the preceding pages. [b] After leading this activity two or three times, allow one or two students to be the leaders. [c] Get written or oral student reactions to the procedure. Do they have suggestions for modifying it in any way? [d] Devote some time to process analysis. How well were task functions carried out? Were there efforts at group maintenance?)

## Three-Step Design

It is difficult to maintain the relative openness and spontaneity of the five-member buzz group when the situation abruptly changes to a twenty-five- or thirty-member discussion. Success in the transition will depend to a great extent on the growth of maturity and the leader skills of the teacher.

In the initial stages, a three-step process may prove helpful in creating a supportive atmosphere for nonparticipators.

1.   This design will take two forty- to fifty-minute class sessions.

2.   The teacher may pass out guide sheets and give instructions a day ahead, or he may do this orienting at the beginning of discussion session one.

3.   Teacher sets the stage by passing out sheets and commenting on questions.

4.   He then tells the class (e.g., twenty-four students) that they may discuss the questions in groups of six for ten minutes.

5.   At the end of ten minutes, the sixes will combine into two groups of twelve for twenty minutes.

6.   At the end of twenty minutes, the groups of twelve will summarize their discussion in written form. (Two written copies will be handed to teacher.)

7. At the following session of the class, the teacher reconvenes the original groups of six for ten minutes, giving each group a copy of the written summaries handed in at the last session of the class.

8. (*Notes:* [a] In this design, the students move more gradually into the total class. [b] On the content level, much work will be done regarding the discussion questions. [c] On the process level, there will be more opportunity for individual participation.)

The teacher should never lose sight of the fact that process awareness and process skills do not occur automatically when people form aggregates of any size. Thus, the student who badly needs support and recognition in order to participate may not be helped very much in a buzz group. In order to help an aggregate grow toward group maturity, the teacher must help the students to be aware of and develop skills in maintenance as well as task functions.[6] In doing this, of course, he should not play down skill development in the task area, since students (from kindergarten through the graduate school) need work in both these sets of functions. (Typically dependent group members tend to supply only initiating behaviors, leaving most of the other task functions to the appointed leader. In the initially unstructured T-Group,[7] members usually feel somewhat lost and helpless when the *Trainer* refuses to take over the stereotype of the chairman role and tell them what to do.)

## Brainstorming

A rather specialized technique has been developed in the higher echelons of the American business world, which involves participants in a sometimes breathless process of tapping the idea reservoir of the group. Designed to facilitate problem solving,

[6] See discussion of task and maintenance functions, pages 72-74 of this book.

[7] For a comprehensive treatment of the T-Group technique of group training see Leland P. Bradford et al., *T-Group Theory and Laboratory Method: Innovation in Reeducation* (New York: Wiley, 1964).

For participation in T-Group Training, contact National Training Laboratories of the National Education Association, Washington, D.C.

the activity of *brainstorming* can easily be adapted to the classroom. The versatility of group brainstorming has been pointed up by Dr. Robert Wilson of Portland State College in Oregon in these words:

> Brainstorming may be used on almost any type of problem. It is especially useful on school and classroom problems such as: What can we do to make our school more interesting and more comfortable? How can we develop better discipline in the playground? How can the line in the lunch room be speeded up? What questions would be most interesting to study in this unit?[8]

Though success with the approach will come only through practice, the basic rules are simple to understand:

1. Group size should be about twelve.
2. Subject matter should be in terms of a specific problem.
3. The problem should be one that could be solved in a number of alternative ways. (An either-or question would not be appropriate.)
4. What is sought is a number of ideas. (Questions calling for judgment are not appropriate.)
5. Quantity is called for initially. (Evaluation of ideas come later.)
6. Criticism of ideas is not permitted. (This will come at a later stage.)
7. Participants should feel completely free to throw out any ideas that occur—even the wildest notion is encouraged.
8. Participants should also feel free to build on the ideas expressed by others or to combine any number of previous ideas. (In the jargon of brainstorming, this is called "piggy-backing" or "hitchhiking.")
9. Participants should be quite familiar with the problem and with at least the traditional ways it or similar problems have been handled in the past.
10. Wherever possible, it is helpful to "seed" the group with a few experienced "brainstormers."

[8] Alex F. Osborn, *Applied Imagination: Principles and Procedures of Creative Problem-Solving* (New York: Charles Scribner's Sons, 1963), p. 163. This book is an excellent resource in the area of brainstorming.

Having spent so much of the time of their lives in school-rooms, students have many feelings about the ways in which classes are conducted and have many ideas for improvement. Unfortunately, independent student thinking is rarely valued by school authority and therefore rarely used by the student. Thus, the brainstorming of ideas may come with difficulty at first and instant success should not be anticipated. If the teacher follows up on the exercise in such a way as to show respect for the ideas proposed, however, subsequent trials will become more productive. A teacher who can reach the storehouse of ideas locked within his students will be rich indeed.

One of the many applications of brainstorming might follow several sessions of student committee work. (Later, as the group becomes more cohesive, the teacher may wish to have the class work on the improvement of *his* teaching, but it may be easier on both parties to begin by having them analyze something *they* have done.) The committee work may be evaluated in a number of ways. Typical of these is the full class discussion led by the teacher who asks, "How can we improve committee work?" The number of ideas volunteered will be related to the freedom felt by individuals in the class to participate openly. Often such a session is limited to the few who characteristically do most of the talking.

An alternative might be to brainstorm the problem, and the procedure might be as follows:

1. At the class session during which the committee work is finished, the teacher announces that the next two sessions of the class will be devoted to the development of ideas that will make committee work more enjoyable and valuable.

2. For homework, each student is to write three ways in which committee work in the class could be improved.

3. At the class session that concludes the current committee work, the teacher leads a brief discussion concerning student feeling about the activity.

4. With this discussion as a motivational springboard, the teacher suggests that what is needed is a boxful of ideas, and that they can, if they wish, play a game of idea production during the next two sessions.

5.  The class is divided into two groups with equal numbers of boys and girls in each group. The groups are labelled A and B.

6.  At the beginning of the next session, the teacher will collect the homework assigned mainly to assure that class members will have done some thinking. The papers are collected because reading from one's paper would destroy the spontaneity of the group session.

7.  Two secretaries are selected for each group, their tasks being to write ideas as they are contributed. One will take the even-numbered ideas while the other will take the odd. This should give them time to keep a running notation in longhand.

8.  Teacher will explain that group A will begin for fifteen minutes with group B as observers. Then the groups will reverse roles so that each group will have fifteen minutes activity during the session.

9.  Rules are that no criticism is allowed. The main purpose is to get out ideas. No idea should be withheld because a person feels it is wild or foolish. Ideas will be judged later. Right now, let's just concentrate on getting them out. It is also part of the game that one may add to the ideas of others or combine two or three ideas into a new one. In this way, the power of the group can be released.

10. Having said this, the teacher seats group A in the center of the room in a circle and, after restating the problem, directs them to begin. (The problem is: "How can we improve committee work in this class?")

11. As the group begins, the teacher may have to "prime the pump" by contributing a few ideas. He may begin with one conservative and one wildly liberal idea, being careful not to dominate the session. The homework assignment should be helpful in getting things started.

12. During the session, the teacher acts to enforce the rule of no criticism and to reinforce the norm of anything goes. It is essential to challenge the habit of idea censorship, which inhibits people from free participation.

13. After fifteen minutes, the teacher will switch groups and continue for a second session.

14. At the end of the class, the teacher (or a student group) can take the lists of the group secretaries and arrange them for duplication. The duplicated list should be ready for the next class.

15. At the next class, idea lists can be given out to each student and, through class discussion, narrowed down to a few usable ideas, one or more of which can be implemented.

For the purposes of group maturity, brainstorming introduces maintenance emphasis in terms of a reduction in critical comments and because of the norm of reinforcing any and all participation. The exercise itself is motivating because it departs from the usual routine and because it tends to involve most of the students. It should be quite productive in terms of ideas, and it should develop student commitment to carrying out the ideas since the students themselves developed them.

## Case Analysis

A highly motivational device on which a class discussion can be built is the case-analysis technique, which has received a good deal of attention and refinement at the Harvard Graduate School of Business Administration. This approach, which can be modified to meet a wide number of classroom objectives, is one of the sharpest attacks yet developed on the "teacher talk-student listen" syndrome of so much current schooling. In conducting a case study, it is the teacher who listens and asks questions; the students define the elements, analyze the problem, propose solutions, and begin to gain confidence in *their* ability to come up with answers.

"A good case is the vehicle by which a chunk of reality is brought into the classroom to be worked over by the class and the instructor."[9] This reality is in the form of a written account of a problem faced by one or more people. Details concerning

[9] Kenneth R. Andrews, ed., *The Case Method of Teaching Human Relations and Administration* (Cambridge, Mass.: Harvard University Press, 1960), p. 215.

those involved are provided plus the background leading up to the moment a decision has to be made. The case description usually ends at that point. The members of the class then face the task of analyzing the data in order to develop one or more possible courses of action.

In this process, the outside reality of the case becomes the inside reality of the class as students begin to identify with the characters and bring their own personal feelings to bear.

> . . . the children analyze the emotional forces involved, isolate and discuss the conflicts and problems of the people, evaluate their personalities. Then . . . they talk about themselves. Have they ever felt these emotions? What have they done about it? Have they ever faced a similar problem? How did they solve it?[10]

Personal involvement leads to a feeling of coping with reality, and this enhances the learnings in problem-solving skills and in the process of critical thinking. In contrast to other teaching procedures, which seek to impart elements of the scientific method in outline form to be memorized and fed back on written tests, the case method follows the concept of "learning by doing."

> In most of the cases, one person has to make a decision at the end of the case. The reader should, after reading the case, assume the *position* of the decision-maker. . . . The reader's job is not to try to decide what (the case character) would have done, but to decide what *he* the reader, would do given the circumstances which have led up to the moment of decision.[11]

True to the aim of providing student experiences that will develop self-direction and personal commitment, the classroom analysis of a written case gives initial guidance and structure, but places the burden of thinking, reacting, and reflecting upon the students, where it belongs. Teaching should not consist of the teacher's demonstrating *his* ability to deal with material,

---

[10] H. Edmund Bullis and Emily E. O'Malley, *Human Relations in the Classroom: Course I* (Wilmington, Delaware: The Delaware State Society for Mental Hygiene, 1954), p. 2.
[11] Harold L. Hodgkinson, *Educational Decisions: A Casebook* (Englewood Cliffs, N.J.: Prentice-Hall, Inc., 1963), pp. x-xi.

but rather in the creation of situations in which students can test out, develop, and evaluate *their* abilities. Typical of student reactions to the case approach are the findings of a study done in teacher training more than thirty years ago. Students involved said:

> Students grow in ability to recognize, analyze, and solve problems in their teaching situations. Students take an active and objective part in their own professional and personal development. Students develop leadership and intelligent followership through the give-and-take relationships set up by this technique.[12]

It should be understood at the outset that case analysis, or any other approach that tends to introduce change in the norm of the active teacher and the passive students, is *not* the easiest road for the teacher to follow. Use of the method does not guarantee instant success (any more than a lecture or recitation approach might). On the positive side, it has the advantage of being a break in the routine most students have come to expect. In addition, it provides initial structuring on which to base a discussion—the student is provided with a focus for his thinking. And if the case presentation touches areas of his personal experience, he can draw on previous thinking and acting in order to participate in discussion. On the negative side, the student is faced with teacher refusal to play the usual game of telling him what he has read, pointing out the more subtle aspects, doing the job of analysis for him, and, finally, telling him the answer. For many students, such an experience is a frustrating one. He has probably had very few learning experiences in which he has really had to think, even fewer in which he has had to interact with his peers, and he may have little confidence that what he says or decides might have validity. A common response after some discussion is a student request that now the teacher tell them the *real* answer.

The teacher's role here, as in every teaching situation, is one of maintaining successfully a delicate balance. On the one hand, he must resist the temptation to give in to dependent

---

[12] D. Henryetta Sperle, *The Case Method Technique in Professional Training* (New York: Bureau of Publications, Teachers College, Columbia University, 1933), p. 66.

students by telling them all the answers (actually, they will not value this type of experience in the long run); on the other hand, he must respond in some helpful way, or increasing anxiety and frustration will diminish student learning. In essence, his goal is to be helpful not in terms of giving answers or doing the students' thinking, but rather in terms of teaching his students how to *get* answers and how to *do* thinking. His goal is a long-range one. At some point, the student will no longer have the teacher to guide him—what will he do then? It is part of our folklore that an American private soldier can and does carry on even when officers and noncommissioned officers have been killed. This claim is often set against the behavior of soldiers from more authoritarian cultures who stand helpless and bewildered when their leaders are taken away. It would be ridiculous to assume that case analysis, or any other teaching method, could magically clear up these problems. If self-direction and the ability to think for one's self is a desirable movement toward solution, however, then this method is one step in the right direction.

Before defining and illustrating case analysis, it would be well to know specifically what the teacher might have in mind when he uses the technique. Following is a list of main emphases, teacher behaviors, and expected outcomes. (The reader should always keep in mind that realistic outcomes of the first experience would be merely that the students learn something about handling such an experience. The general outcomes will probably not be realized until they have repeated the experience several times.)

## Main Emphasis

In using case analysis, the teacher will be concerned with the following:

1.  Deepening and extending subject-matter learning.
2.  Student application of previous learnings.
3.  Development of skills in critical thinking.
4.  Application to subsequent learning.

**Teacher behaviors.** In conducting a case-analysis session, the teacher will:

1. Be nondirective in leading discussion.
2. Help students to "see" their approach to dealing with the problem.
3. Point out task and maintenance functions.
4. Help students see relationships between what they are doing now and previous learnings in the content of the course and in processes of thinking, problem solving, and decision making. (Where a case is used as an introduction, this point would have to be modified.)
5. Help them determine what further knowledge and understandings they need and what methods of inquiry (reading, researching, interviewing, field trips, guest speakers, etc.) they might use to gain this further knowledge and understanding.
6. Help them to summarize and analyze what they have done with their discussion of the case on both content and process levels.

**Expected outcomes.** As a result of participating in case analysis, students will:

1. Develop more self-direction and willingness to share responsibility for learning with the teacher.
2. Display increasing skill in critical thinking, problem solving, and decision making.
3. Modify their attitudes toward the subject matter of the case under discussion.
4. Increasingly apply previous learnings in dealing with present problems.
5. Demonstrate increasing ability to analyze their interactions on both content and process levels. (What have we learned about the subject? What have we learned about improving group problem solving and decision making?)
6. Become motivated toward further learning.

7. Display increasing confidence in the importance and validity of their own decisions.

Procedure for the case technique includes having students read the case before the discussion session. At the beginning of the session, the teacher opens with a question such as, "What do you see as the problem here?" or "Who would like to begin the discussion?" From that point, he acts to supply needed task or maintenance functions when they are not forthcoming from the students. He does this infrequently and only as a model for the students to pick up and use. It is *their* problem; *their* discussion. The teacher avoids being maneuvered into the role of question answerer or decision maker. While this may be difficult for him and for the students at first, the teacher's attitude of careful listening and his willingness to participate in a clarifying and idea-linking manner soon begins to set a norm for participation. After all, the students learned present behaviors such as note-taking and recitation from their teachers.

Certainly there should be a structure for the discussion and the development of a solution or solutions. The question raised in case analysis is whether the source of structure should be the teacher or the students. Of course, this is not really an either-or-question. While the teacher, using a case approach, does not supply initial structure, he *does* do everything he can to help students to learn the process of structuring for themselves.

Case analysis may be adapted to a wide variety of teacher objectives in any subject area. For example:

| | |
|---|---|
| *Art:* | Decision concerning paintings which should be hung on the walls of the school. |
| *Business:* | Decision on the introduction of a new office practice. |
| *Driver Education:* | Decision on the background events leading to an accident. |
| *English:* | Decision concerning poetic experience in everyday life. |
| *Foreign Language:* | Discussion concerning reluctance to speak a foreign language for fear of sounding silly or foolish. |

| | |
|---|---|
| *Home Economics:* | Decision concerning career women versus housewives. |
| *Home Room:* | Decision concerning variance in teacher and student views on selection of candidates for student council election. |
| *Industrial Arts:* | Decision on craftsmanship versus planned obsolescence in industrial processes. |
| *Mathematics:* | Decision on use of deductive versus inductive method of learning mathematics. |
| *Music:* | Decision concerning emphasis on popular music versus emphasis on classical music. |
| *Physical Education (Health):* | Decision concerning harmful effects of smoking. |
| *Science:* | Decision on fluoridation of water supply. |
| *Social Studies:* | Decision on use of public welfare monies and policies for those on relief. |

Following is an illustration of a case study as it might be used in a foreign language classroom. The first paragraph introduces the teacher and sets up the problem. Paragraph two provides background on the teacher and on how she views the job of teaching. It also adds some data concerning her reactions to certain students.

---

*Case Study*

INSTRUCTIONS:

Read this case study carefully. Then read it again. Try to get the situation clearly in mind and the behavior and attitudes of people involved. Can you put yourself in the position of the teacher? Of one of the students? How will this situation develop? What would you do if

---

you were involved as one of the people discussed or as one of the other students?

*Parlez-Vous Français?*

Miss Johnson is a teacher of French at Harrington High School. She is liked by the better students in her classes because she knows her subject well, speaks French fluently, and is very much interested in having her students speak it well. Her less able students, however, feel uneasy in her class because of the pressure to speak often in the language. Their defense is to never volunteer, take a long time in answering, and then say as few words as possible. Miss Johnson does not want to call on the better students all the time, but it is obvious that she is unhappy with the response of the others in the class.

She was able to travel in France for a year with her parents when she was a high school student, and she has visited the country twice while a student at college. She loves the language and is quite strict about her students' pronunciation. She can't understand anyone who does not share her enthusiasm for the language, and the students who won't even try to speak fluently upset her. Though she tries to hide it, she becomes frustrated and angry when students reply to a ten-word question with, "Oui."

Lewis Stanton is one of the less fluent students in Miss Johnson's third-period class, and he feels that she should leave him alone. For the past week, he feels she has been picking on him and trying to embarrass him by asking him questions in French. He doesn't mind studying the stuff and taking tests, but he feels sort of silly trying to speak. It's a sort of sissy thing to do, and he is a football player.

Miss Johnson is looking forward to Thursday's class. She has been working on Lewis Stanton, one of her more reluctant students, for a week, and she feels she is beginning to reach him. All he needs is a little more pressure, and he will begin to speak the language more spontaneously.

The Thursday class, however, does not go so well. Miss Johnson calls on Lewis several times, and he hangs his head and mumbles. Even when she asks him sharply to speak up, it does no good, and the class is beginning to show the tension. Finally, the bell rings, and the class members race for the door.

After class, Lewis meets Mary Howard and Sam Fenton, two of his classmates.

*Lewis:*   I'm fed up.

*Mary:*   What are you complaining about now?

*Lewis:*   What am I complaining about now? French is what I'm complaining about now.

*Sam:*   You don't parlez-vous?

*Lewis:*   It's all right for you to talk. Miss Johnson leaves you alone.

*Mary:*   You think she's picking on you?

*Lewis:*   Isn't it obvious?

*Mary:*   Oh, I don't know. I think she wants you to learn.

*Lewis:*   If she'd leave me alone, maybe I could.

*Sam:*   Maybe you ought to make more of an effort.

*Lewis:*   But I feel sort of foolish speaking French. It sounds so phoney.

*Mary:*   It's a beautiful language.

*Lewis:*   Yeah. Maybe for girls.

*Sam:*   Well, what can you do?

*Lewis:*   I'll tell you what I can do. I can go see the guidance counselor.

*Sam:*   Yeah, I suppose you could do that.

*Mary:*   I think you're being sort of childish. Why don't you talk to Miss Johnson?

*Lewis:*   Oh no you don't. I don't want to fail the course.

*Sam:*   You know, you may have something there.

> Maybe a bunch of us ought to go to the guidance counselor.
>
> *Mary:*   Oh, you're both terrible.
>
> *Sam:*   Well, what would you suggest?
>
> *Mary:*   We could bring it up in class.
>
> *Lewis:*   I don't know, Mary.
>
> *Mary:*   I think that's the only fair thing for Miss Johnson. She's really a very nice person.
>
> *Sam:*   On the other hand, we could just wear her down by not volunteering.
>
> *Lewis:*   I don't know what to do, but I feel like doing something.

Paragraph three brings a student into the picture along with *his* reactions to the situation. The next two paragraphs set up a confrontation between teacher and student, and the following dialogue builds toward a decision-making moment. After the students have had an opportunity to read through the case, they may begin their discussion. Some points that they may bring out would include the following:

*Miss Johnson*
Personally interested and knowledgeable in subject.
Wants students to speak fluently and with exact pronunciation.
Is impatient with inhibited students.
Feels that pressure is helpful.
Sometimes speaks sharply to students.
Seems like a "nice person" to Mary.

*Lewis Stanton*
One of less fluent students.
Feels picked on.
Athlete.
Feels speaking is sissy.
Wants to go to guidance counselor.

*General Situation*
Feelings concerning speaking a foreign language.

Methods of teaching.

Teacher-Student communication.

While the points above will probably be brought out in a discussion of the case, it is most possible that other, more unexpected, points will be raised. While the teacher will have and should have specific objectives in choosing or writing a case study, he should also be alert to additional areas that students bring up as they project their own feelings into the discussion. As all sensitive teachers do in any teaching situation, the instructor using the case-analysis method will wish to define and clarify any bypaths that may be brought up by the students.

## In General

The exercises and approaches outlined in this chapter may be used separately or in support of each other to provide a stepping stone toward open communication in the classroom. Like any teaching methods, they should be a means of reaching the teacher's objectives. Actually, any teaching, call it traditional, progressive, or any other name, seeks to create a readiness and an ability to learn. Teaching without the creation of these conditions is similar to a book in the hands of an illiterate.

# chapter 5

# Reaction and Evaluation Instruments

In the conceptual framework of Chapter 2 as well as in the various exercises suggested in Chapter 4, stress has been placed on group growth and development in the classroom. Teacher efforts to foster a movement from aggregate to group are justified because they should result in (1) personal relevance in student learning, (2) high levels of student participation and self-direction, (3) student assumption of concern and responsibility for reinforcement of appropriate behavior in the classroom, and (4) *affective* as well as *cognitive* learning. Movement toward maturity as a group becomes ultimately the responsibility of each member (teacher is a member), and all members become involved in continual assessment and modification of learning activities. Relating this to the framework on pages 40-41, a learning aggregate begins with the backgrounds that participants bring to the first session plus the initial structure, moves into interaction and initial efforts to establish norms of behavior, reacts to and tries out these norms, and comes to accept certain ways of working together. All this results in behavior change which is the modification of initial member backgrounds and classroom structure. This behavior change will be recycled through II, III, and IV to produce further change which will be again recycled.

| I | | II | | III | | IV | |
|---|---|---|---|---|---|---|---|
| (a) | (b) | (c) | (d) | (e) | (f) | (g) | (h) |
| Participant Background | Aggregate Structure | Inter-action | Norm Inputs | Reactions | Try-Out Behaviors | Norm Accep-tance | Behavior Change |

Teachers should be aware that while behavior change (modification of initial situation) is bound to occur, it may be negative rather than positive. Teacher and students may learn to hate or be apathetic toward school; they may learn better ways to alienate each other rather than form a cohesive group; students may learn better ways to "butter up" or torment the teacher; and the teacher may learn better ways to use stern, repressive methods of "discipline." In the cognitive domain, facts and concepts may be learned by rote rather than understanding, relating, internalizing, and using. In the affective domain, emotions may be submerged to later surface as problems in motivation and discipline rather than being brought out in the open to be examined, confronted, and resolved.

The often heard cognitive teacher's request that students ask questions—even "stupid" questions—so that he will know where they are confused and thus be able to teach them better is a request for honesty. This same request needs to be repeated in the affective area by asking that students state how they are feeling about themselves, the activities of the class, and the other members, including the teacher. It is interesting to note the interplay between *cognitive* and *affective* aspects in the first question above. Why wouldn't a student risk asking a "stupid" question? He probably would if the risk weren't too great. The question is a *cognitive* item; the risk feeling is *affective*. It can, thus, be seen that *cognitive* (content level) communication is affected by *affective* (process level) concerns. Process-level as well as content-level skills, then, need to be developed if learning is to be maximized.

Feedback (III: e and f) and increasing skill in both giving and receiving it become vital in this theory of learning. Such feedback involves reacting to initial normative behavior, evaluating, suggesting modifications, and trying out modifications. Changes might include speaking out rather than raising hands, sitting in a circle rather than in rows, working part of the class time in subgroups rather than as a whole class, and/or expressing both positive and negative feelings spontaneously. Trying out of modifications could result in returning to old norms, maintaining the new because they seem successful, or making further changes.

Making and testing changes in ways of operating the class (III: e and f) depend for success on the readiness and willingness of teacher and students to participate in the evaluation of class activities. In addition, it involves the development of instruments and techniques for the gathering of data. This inclusion of students, in itself, is a norm modification since even cognitive evaluation has rested traditionally on teacher-made and standardized tests. Certainly improvements could be made in the cognitive area, but this chapter—and the book—will focus on *process* evaluation.

## Purposes of Process Evaluation

Simply put, *evaluation* is a way of assessing the attainment of objectives, though it may sometimes also be a means of developing them. As a normal course of affairs, teachers plan and carry out plans by (1) deciding on content, objectives, and approach; (2) developing classroom—and out of class—experiences; and (3) using observation, pen-and-paper tests, and other data-gathering procedures in order to determine the extent to which their teaching and the students' learning has succeeded.

According to the theoretical framework of pages 40-41, the products of evaluation would be fed back to the students (perhaps *by* the students) in order to focus attention on whatever change has taken place as a result of classroom interaction. This, in turn, would influence the direction, the kind, and the quality of further learning experiences as indicated by the *Cycling Process* of the framework. Inherent in this concept of teaching and learning is that student involvement in the evaluation is, in itself, an important learning activity.

Stemming from this way of viewing evaluation of learning, five purposes of evaluation may be identified: These are:

1. To get evidence that objectives are being achieved.
2. To help students improve self-assessment skills.
3. To obtain data for analysis.

4. To feed analyzed data back into the social system of the classroom.

5. To improve the quality of classroom interaction and, therefore, of learning.

## Data-Gathering Instruments

All the instruments illustrated and discussed on the following pages have been used successfully in practice and can be used by teachers in their present forms. It should be kept in mind, however, that these instruments were developed in relation to specific objectives (Purposes: #1), and that they can and should be modified to fit the objectives of anyone wishing to employ them. They should also be shared with students who may be involved in their use (Purposes: #2). This would require not only that students respond to the instruments, but that they themselves (perhaps through a student committee) collect the responses, summarize them, report the results to the class, and move toward skills in developing their own instruments in the future.

Several conditions must be met in order that process evaluation successfully develop useful data for analysis (Purposes: #3). First, an atmosphere of mutual trust needs to be developed between students and teacher. If it does not, the students will treat the instruments as a game in which they must tell the teacher what he seems to want to hear, and the teacher, on his part, will be reluctant to share the results of the instruments. Second, the teacher must be open to the possibilities of learning about himself. Although his role differs in many ways from that of the students, he is also a participating group member and, as such, influences the process going on in the class. Third, he must support action to be taken in response to the data (Purposes: #4). And fourth, he must help his students to see that process evaluation is not merely a focus on the teacher's teaching, but that it also includes a scrutiny of the learner's learning. A critical analysis of what is going on in the classroom should deal with learner behavior as well as teacher activity. It seems helpful to repeat the stress on the term *interaction* when dealing with process. A really successful classroom situation depends on *both* teacher and students (Purposes: #5).

Though many research designs are possible,[1] three approaches can be identified in relation to the beginning, the middle, and the end of a learning experience. The first of these would involve the gathering of data at the beginning (a policy rarely followed in traditional schooling) so that it may be compared with later data in order to determine change. The second design would be to dip occasionally into the ongoing process in order to find out how things are going so that any necessary corrective measures can be taken. The third design is the traditional final examination where the learning experience as a whole is summarized and evaluated.

## Two-Step Design

Essentially, this procedure consists of measuring what exists before a learning experience, going through the experience, and measuring it again at the end. If there is appreciable gain in terms of the teacher's objectives when the second measure is taken it may be assumed that it is due to the learning that has taken place. Without the initial measurement, one has no clearcut data on the state of affairs at the beginning. Where this data does not exist, there may be a question about a high scorer on a final measurement. Did he score high because of the instruction or because he knew the material when he entered the course?

An effective instrument for a two-step design measuring process is the agree-disagree exercise discussed on pages 139-141. As an illustration, suppose that the teacher develops objectives in terms of (1) increasing student participation, (2) involving students in course planning, and (3) increasing students' interest in the subject matter. One vital ingredient in the attainment of these objectives is student attitude, and an agree-disagree exercise could be constructed with pro and con statements that would give a clear picture of beginning student attitudes. Administration of the same statements at the end of the learning experience would provide data showing whether the learning

[1] See Matthew B. Miles, *Learning to Work in Groups* (New York: Bureau of Publications, Teachers College, Columbia University, 1959), Chapter 8, "Evaluating Training," pp. 223-52. See also Claire Sellitz et al., *Research Methods in Social Relations* (New York: Holt, 1959).

had altered student attitudes and to what degree. A similar measurement could be made for any set of teacher (or teacher-student) objectives. If this were done for a three-week experience, the data could be shared with the class in order to pinpoint the reasons why there was or was not change in attitudes and what further activities should be carried on in light of the data.

If, for example, there was positive change in all three, it might be helpful to continue similar classroom approaches. On the other hand, if one or more showed no change or negative change, some investigation and analysis would seem called for. If the problem were centered in student involvement in course planning, probing questions would be, "What is causing the difficulty?" and "What can we do to improve the situation?" Following the implementation of decisions made, a third instrument might be given at the end of the sixth week to determine whether changes in classroom operation have produced any changes in attitudes.

Sociometric techniques,[2] which attempt to chart the relationships of students in the classroom, may also be used in a before-and-after look at process. This technique involves gathering data on student acceptance (and sometimes rejection) of peers, and the charting or diagramming of these feelings. The teacher, then, has a graphic record of those students most accepted, those most ignored, those rejected, and what dyadic or subgroup relationships exist in terms of mutual choice and acceptance. Data is generally gathered by asking the class to list, on a first- second- and third-choice basis, students they would want to invite to a class party and to indicate the student they would most like to exclude. This data is then placed on a single sheet of paper with circles and squares representing students and connecting lines with arrows indicating choices. If one imagines a class of seven girls and eight boys asked to make three choices apiece, the data would be assembled as in F*gure 14, and the diagram would look like Figure 15.

From the Figure 14 data, one can see that the boys relate (or say they relate) only to the boys and the girls only to the

───────────────────────

[2] See Norman E. Gronlund, *Sociometry in the Classroom* (New York: Harper, 1959). Also Helen H. Jennings et al., *Sociometry in Group Relations* (Washington, D.C.: American Council on Education, 1948). Also Jacob L. Moreno, *Who Shall Survive?* (New York: Beacon House, 1958).

girls with one exception. Rich is the second choice of three girls, and he has chosen Mary as *his* third choice. Gert seems to be the center of attraction for the girls since five out of six chose her in first position. Betty did not choose her, but then no one chose Betty. Her choice of Rich may have to do with her first choice of Mary, who seems to have an interrelationship with Rich. It should be stressed that such interpretation of the data must be supported by observation of classroom behavior. The sociogram is only a supplement to the teacher's general feeling for classroom process. However, it does pinpoint relationships, and it often reveals situations not so apparent to the teacher in general classroom operation.

Except for Betty, the girls seem to have a fairly cohesive group with Gert as its focus and, probably, its leader. Iris may be a bit of an outsider since she was chosen only once and that was Dot's *third* choice.

The boys seem to be formed more into subgroups. Rich, Mike, and Pete are a triad, and Tom and Sam form a dyad. While all members of the triad are chosen at least once by the others, Sam and Tom receive only a single vote and that is the third choice of John, who is himself isolated from the group.

### SOCIOMETRIC CHOICES

| Names | First Choice | Second Choice | Third Choice |
|-------|--------------|---------------|--------------|
| John  | Vern  | Fred  | Tom   |
| Fred  | Mike  | Vern  | Pete  |
| Mike  | Rich  | Pete  | Fred  |
| Pete  | Mike  | Rich  | Vern  |
| Rich  | Mike  | Pete  | Mary  |
| Vern  | Fred  | Mike  | Rich  |
| Sam   | Tom   | Vern  | Rich  |
| Tom   | Sam   | Vern  | Rich  |
| Gert  | Clara | Dot   | Mary  |
| Clara | Gert  | Dot   | Jane  |
| Jane  | Gert  | Rich  | Clara |
| Mary  | Gert  | Rich  | Clara |
| Betty | Mary  | Rich  | Clara |
| Dot   | Gert  | Clara | Iris  |
| Iris  | Gert  | Dot   | Jane  |

Figure 14

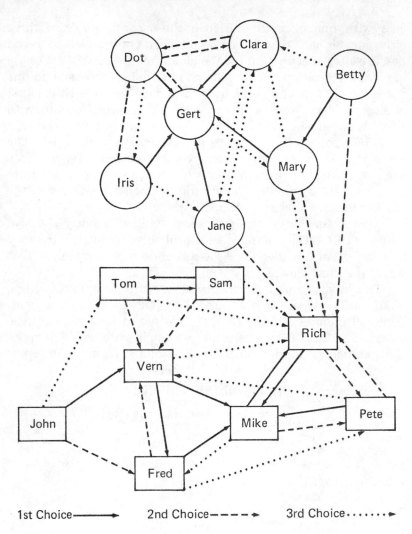

1st Choice⟶        2nd Choice⟶        3rd Choice·······⟶

Figure 15. Sociogram

Vern may be the group leader except that there may not be much group feeling among the boys to support him. It is interesting that the Tom-Sam dyad votes for him second. But they vote for Rich third, and his support by Mike, Pete, Jane, Mary, and Betty may mean something in terms of his leadership potential. Fred—chosen by Vern, John, and Mike—may be a strong independent force. John, like Betty, has not been chosen by anyone. If the teacher has allowed students to sit where they please in class, it would be interesting to check the sociogram against the seating chart.

The imaginative teacher can use sociometric techniques in a number of ways. It is, for example, helpful to know at the beginning of a course who knows whom among the students and how well they know each other. For this purpose, a sheet such as that shown in Figure 16 may be passed out to the class during the first week and a composite picture made as in Figure 17.

The data-gathering sheet shown below in Figure 16 yields a number of choices that can be plotted to form a composite picture as in Figure 17 below. This gives the teacher a quick, clear image of who knows whom and who are strangers in the class. Figure 17 shows a group in which there are few close

*First Street School*

*Section 8—4*                                                            *Miss Daniels*

Instructions: Using the list of your classmates below, indicate by placing an X in the appropriate space which students you know well, slightly, or not at all.

My name is _____.

| Class List | Know Well | Know Slightly | Know Not at All |
|---|---|---|---|
| Mary J. | | | X |
| Jane P. | | | X |
| Freda R. | | | X |
| Harriet Q. | | X | |
| John H. | | | |
| Michael B. | | | X |
| Frederick S. | | X | |
| James T. | | | X |

**Figure 16.** Data-Gathering Sheet

friendships and in which most students do not know each other. It is interesting that while Mary is close to both Jane and Harriet, the latter two girls do not indicate that they know each other. Fred and Mike are close, and Fred indicates that he knows most of the people in the class slightly. With the exception of Freda, however, they do not indicate that they know Fred. Freda, while she has no close friends in this class, seems to know most of the students and they seem to know her. James feels that he knows no one at all, but Harriet and Fred feel that they know him slightly. This beginning measurement can be compared to a second taken a month later. The numbers will probably shift somewhat to the left no matter what approach the teacher uses since proximity through time helps people to at least identify faces, and relationships may be pursued out of class in clubs, on the playground, or in the lunchroom. In time, students make at least surface contact with those sitting near them. If the teacher actively seeks group growth and student involvement, however, and if he is successful, there should be an appreciable shift to the left. A record will also exist of those individual students who remain unknowing and unknown.

Data such as that diagrammed in Figure 15 is useful for the teacher, but it may be difficult to share with the class, at least in the beginning stages. As mutual trust grows, however, students will become more able to deal with their mutual feelings openly and more able to express them in ways which help rather than hurt others.

The intragroup relationships data of Figure 17, however, may be shared immediately, and the students can become involved in the planning of ways to increase their knowledge of each other. It has been the experience of the author that students in classes from the elementary through the graduate school do not ordinarily become acquainted with each other in the classroom setting in ways that help them to understand each other and to develop ways of relating. Students *do*, however, develop feelings about each other that affect their learning and the general atmosphere of the class. Often, such feelings tend to be negative, but there is no way to deal with feelings in class situations that stress content levels and ignore process. It is, to a large extent, the near impossibility of dealing with feelings con-

*Composite Picture of Intragroup Relationships, Section 8—4*

Date _____

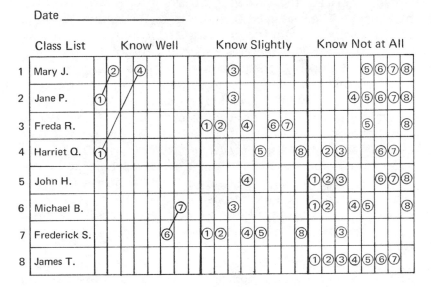

Figure 17

structively in the average classroom that causes behavior "problems" with the more extroverted students, withdrawal of the more introverted, and premature school leaving on the part of those who tend most to need the schooling experience.

The premise that intragroup relationships, if fostered in the classroom, will enhance learning seems reasonable enough. However, many teachers, brought up themselves in a highly formal manner, are suspicious of any activities that seem irrelevant to the learning of subject matter. They are quite right to be suspicious. Hopefully, of course, they will not use suspicion as an excuse for unwillingness to try new ideas. The collection and analysis of data such as suggested in Figure 17 needs to be done to determine the growth, if any, of intragroup relations. This, in turn, must be checked against measurement of growth in student motivation and subject-matter achievement. If growth in these latter has occurred and it can be related to growth in group relations, then work on group relations will be seen as a desirable school activity.

## The Gathering of Data

Printed forms for the gathering of group ratings or reactions are, or should be, designed to move from the simple question, "How are we doing?" in the direction of more specific analysis of the situation. This requires a careful definition of precisely what information is needed. An overall reaction on a reactionnaire instrument is similar to a composite grade on a comprehensive test. It is helpful in making generalizations, but it is *not* so helpful in pinpointing deficiency areas or in specifying areas that should be improved. In general, then, the printed data gathering form may begin by asking for an overall rating, but it should also include specific questions in specific areas that seem important to the investigator. Where the investigator is interested in student perceptions of the overall experience, an alternative procedure would be to provide five blank lines and require that the student indicate what *he* sees as the specific areas.

Instruments may be *closed end* (where the respondent is asked merely to check a box or circle a number) or *open end* (where the request is for a general comment or an amplification of a previous rating). Closed-end items yield data that can be expressed in clear-cut terms such as percentages. It makes for quick and easy communication to be able to read back group responses in terms such as YES 76 percent; NO 15 percent; UNDECIDED 9 percent. Where directions call for circling a number on a 1 to 9 continuum with 1 low and 9 high, data can be reported on this item in a class of thirty as:

| (1) | (2) | (3) | (4) | (5) | (6) | (7) | (8) | (9) |
|-----|-----|-----|-----|-----|-----|-----|-----|-----|
| 1   | 3   | 6   | 8   | 4   | 5   | 3   |     |     |

Open-end items call for student expression of opinion, reasons behind the opinion, or suggestions for improvement. This type response is more difficult to report because it is less rigidly controlled by the instrument. Open-end responses can be, however, quite valuable in the interpretation of quantified data. They serve as specific clues to the interpretation of the 15 percent NO or 9 percent UNDECIDED responses, and, of course, they allow the respondents to suggest ways of improvement in their own terms. A middle ground in this area would be first to list five approaches to improvement and have respondents check one or more. Then, in addition, there could be two or three blank spaces for suggestions that do not already appear on the instrument.

Three principles should guide the progress of process evaluation: (1) the teacher should increase his sophistication in the construction of and use of data-gathering instruments; (2) as the class goes on, students should be helped to develop their own instruments; and (3) as the level of trust grows in the class group, there should be a movement toward the open sharing of feelings and opinions so that the crutch of unsigned opinionnaires becomes less necessary.

The following instruments, while they certainly can be used in their present forms, are offered as illustrations of data-gathering methods. As the teacher gains ease and experience, he will want to develop his own instruments keyed to the objectives he and his students have in a particular situation. Items below have been grouped under observation, reaction, self-ratings, and ratings of others.

## Structured Observation

A number of guides for observing and reporting on people in interaction have been developed through the years. They range from simple open-end instructions (observer constructs and writes responses) as in figures 7 through 11 of the present text to more complicated closed-end categories (observer checks one of many already constructed responses) such as figures 18 through 20 which follow. Use of such checklists allows the observer to be more precise in his analysis of what happened. Categories, of course, are prescriptive as well as descriptive. That is, they focus on certain specific aspects of interaction and infer that these are of most significance. As in all prescriptions, stated or inferred, that appear in this book, the reader should make the following instruments his own by (1) changing wording so that categories have personal meaning to him, and (2) noting phenomena which do not seem to fit existing categories and creating his own where he feels it is necessary.

Interaction analysis categories are a good case in point.

## FLANDERS CATEGORIES FOR INTERACTION ANALYSIS[3]

| | | | |
|---|---|---|---|
| TEACHER TALK | INDIRECT INFLUENCE | 1. | *Accepts feeling:* accepts and clarifies student feelings in nonthreatening manner. Predicts or recalls feelings both positive and negative. |
| | | 2. | *Praises or encourages:* praises or encourages student behavior. Uses humor to release tension, but never at the expense of others. Nods head, says "um hum" or "go on." |
| | | 3. | *Accepts or uses ideas of students:* clarifies, builds on, or develops student ideas. (May shift to category 5.) |
| | | 4. | *Asks questions:* asks questions about content or procedures with the expectation that students will answer. |
| | DIRECT INFLUENCE | 5. | *Lecturing:* giving facts or opinions about content or procedure; expressing his own ideas; asking rhetorical questions. |
| | | 6. | *Giving directions:* directions, commands, or orders. |
| | | 7. | *Criticizing or justifying authority:* statements intended to change student behavior to more acceptable pattern; bawling someone out; stating why he is doing what he is doing in a defensive manner. |
| STUDENT TALK | | 8. | *Student talk-response:* talk by students in response to teacher. (Teacher has initiated this exchange.) |
| | | 9. | *Student talk-initiation:* talk by students which *they* initiate. (May include teacher calling on student only when this is teacher's response to student's desire to speak. Otherwise, category 4.) |
| | | 10. | *Silence or confusion:* pauses, short periods of silence in which communication is blocked or unclear. |

There is NO scale implied by these numbers. Each number is intended to classify. It designates a particular kind of communication event. To write these numbers down during an observation is merely to enumerate, not to judge on a value scale.

Figure 18

[3] See E. J. Amidon and Ned A. Flanders, *The Role of the Teacher in the Classroom* (Minneapolis: Association for Productive Teaching, 1957), p. 14. This book is most helpfully specific in charting the verbal give and take of the classroom.

Flanders' work in the fifties (see Figure 18) dealt with seven inferred teacher intents, two types of student input, and confused or unclear moments of silence. Since the categories were developed to label teacher and student classroom talk, it is interesting to see the overwhelming teacher domination reflected in a seven-to-two ratio of teacher/student talk. Even the two areas left for students contain only *one in which the student initiates*—the other is merely response to the teacher's initiation.

Interesting, too, in terms of *affect* are categories of accepting feelings and praising and encouraging. But there is no place to record teacher expression of his own feelings or *student* acceptance of *teacher* feelings. As is usually the case with leader dominance and indirect expression of feeling, teacher anger is expressed as bawling out students (category #7) rather than, "I am angry because you two are talking while I am talking" (no category). Naturally, there is no category to record the student bawling out the teacher (student initiated talk—#9—is not differentiated). Rather than anyone bawling out anyone, it would be good to hear teacher and students sharing feelings and attempting to resolve them. The reader of this book who wants to develop his classroom group might include such new categories to see how often this type behavior occurs compared to teacher scolding.

These comments are in no way a criticism of the categories of Flanders or others. They are intended to point up the prevalence of teacher domination and the absence of straightforward expression of feeling that seems to characterize so many classrooms. If teacher effort to form a group in the classroom were the norm, then other categories would show up. Lack of categories describing expression of personal feeling other than fatherly or motherly teacher reward for "good" behavior is also not a criticism but a challenge.

Lohman, Ober, and Hough[4] have modified Flanders' system on the cognitive level by adding two categories to teacher talk and further differentiating student talk.

[4] E. E. Lohman, R. Ober, and J. B. Hough, "A Study of the Effect of Preservice Training in Interaction Analysis on the Verbal Behavior of Student Teachers," in Edmund J. Amidon and John B. Hough, eds., *Interaction Analysis: Theory, Research, and Application* (Reading, Mass.: Addison-Wesley Publishing Co., 1967), pp. 348-49.

| Teacher Talk | Description of Verbal Behavior |
|---|---|
| New #6 | *Answers student questions:* direct answers to questions regarding content or procedure asked by students. |
| New #9 | *Corrective feedback:* telling a student that his answer is wrong when the incorrectness of the answer can be established by other than opinion, i.e., empirical validation, definition, or custom. |

Student talk is elaborated somewhat, and there is a differentiation of teacher questions (narrow and broad).

| Student Talk | Description of Verbal Behavior |
|---|---|
| New #10 | *Student talk-response:* talk by students in response to requests or narrow teacher questions. The teacher initiates the contact or solicits student's statement. |
| New #11 | *Student talk emitted:* talk by students in response to broad teacher questions which require judgment or opinion. Student declarative statements emitted but not called for by teacher questions. |
| New #12 | *Student question:* questions concerning content or procedure that are directed to the teacher. |

Teachers, in this modified instrument, then, are seen as answering as well as asking questions and as correcting errors unemotionally as well as bawling students out or justifying a stand. Even more important, students are seen as answering both *narrow* teacher questions calling for brief factual responses and *broad* teacher questions calling for student judgment or opinion. Finally, students are seen as questioning the teacher as well as being questioned by him. All this suggests a movement from passive to active learners and a climate in which the teacher is not the only one to do thinking, directing, and questioning.

Another framework for the analysis of interaction balances teacher and student input still further. "The Reciprocal Category System (RCS) . . . [is] an attempt to direct more attention to the variety of student talk that occurs in the classroom. . . . By learning to use the Reciprocal Category System . . . the teacher not only becomes more aware of his own verbal teaching behavior, but he also becomes more aware of the verbal behavior of his students."[5]

This quote serves to emphasize the present author's contention that the student of interaction analysis should learn not only a sophisticated way of assessing classroom verbalizations, but also a sense of what kinds of verbalizations should go on. While the RCS system (Figure 19) shows some similarity to the Flanders, the wider span of student talk, the notions of "warming" and "cooling" the climate, and category #3 for behavior that amplifies and builds on the contributions of others seem important steps forward.

Numbers 1 and 9, respectively, describe behaviors that open up and close down the contributions of others. Of all the categories, these two display most overtly a recognition that feelings as well as facts and ideas are present in the classroom, and the presence or absence of verbalized feeling shows up clearly when categories are placed on a grid for analysis.

Though it is not the purpose of this book to instruct the reader in methods of interaction analysis (for greater detail the reader may consult those entries marked with an asterisk in the bibliography), a few words may be helpful to the reader at this point. Steps in using RCS (Figure 19) are as follows:

1. A trained observer is present as teacher and students interact verbally in the classroom setting.

2. He records each verbalization made by writing the appropriate number of a category in the system.

3. He writes these numbers one below the other, beginning and ending each observation with the number 10 to indicate

[5] Richard L. Ober, Ernest L. Bentley, and Edith Miller, *Systematic Observation of Teaching* (Englewood Cliffs, N.J.: Prentice-Hall, Inc., 1971), pp. 37-38.

*The Reciprocal Category System*[6]

| Category Number Assigned to Teacher Talk | Category Number Assigned to Student Talk |
|---|---|

### Description of Verbal Behavior

1   *"Warms" (informalizes) the climate:* Tends to open   11
up and/or eliminate the tension of the situation;
praises or encourages the action, behavior, comments, ideas, and/or contributions of another;
jokes that release tension not at the expense of
others; accepts and clarifies the feeling tone of
another in a friendly manner. (Feelings may be
positive or negative; predicting or recalling the
feelings of another are included.)

2   *Accepts:* Accepts the action, behavior, comments,   12
ideas, and/or contributions of another; *positive
reinforcement* of these.

3   *Amplifies the contributions of another:* Asks for   13
clarification of, builds on, and/or develops the
action, behavior, comments, ideas, and/or contributions of another.

4   *Elicits:* Asks a question or requests information about   14
the content, subject, or procedure being con-
sidered with the intent that another should
answer (respond).

5   *Responds:* Gives direct answer or response to ques-   15
tions or requests for information that are initiated by another; includes answers to one's own
questions.

6   *Initiates:* Presents facts, information, and/or opinion   16
concerning the content, subject, or procedures
being considered that are self-initiated; expresses

Figure 19 *(Cont. on page 179)*

[6] Ober et al., *Systematic Observation of Teaching*, p. 39.

one's own ideas; lectures (includes rhetorical questions—not intended to be answered).

7   *Directs:* Gives directions, instructions, orders, and/or   17
    assignments to which another is expected to comply.

8   *Corrects:* Tells another that his answer or behavior   18
    is inappropriate or incorrect.

9   *"Cools" (formalizes) the climate:* Makes statements   19
    intended to modify the behavior of another from an inappropriate to an appropriate pattern; may tend to create a certain amount of tension (i.e., bawling out someone, exercising authority in order to gain or maintain control of the situation, rejecting or criticizing the opinion or judgment of another).

10  *Silence or confusion:* Pauses, short periods of silence,   20
    and periods of confusion in which communication cannot be understood by the observer.

**Figure 19**

the opening and the closing of the interchange. (In RCS, #10 indicates silence or confusion.) Brackets indicate paired interaction.

$$\begin{array}{l} \phantom{xxxxxx}10 \\ \phantom{xxxxxxxx}1 \end{array}] \text{ 1st pair}$$

2nd pair [ 12
                6 ] 3rd pair

4th pair [ 13
                5 ] 5th pair

6th pair [ 14
             etc. ] 7th pair
                10

4.  When the observation is concluded, the observer plots pairs on a matrix. The first number of a pair is the row (horizontal) and second is the column (vertical). Pairs in #3 above are 10-1, 1-12, 12-6, 6-13, 13-5, 5-14, and 14-10.

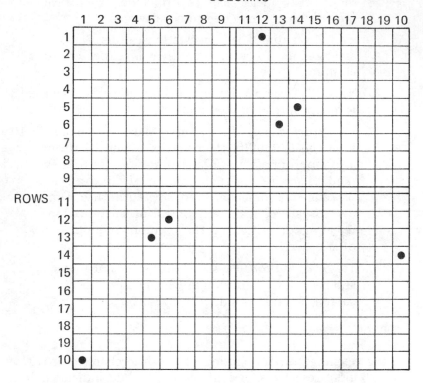

5. After charting, a number of fairly accurate inferences can be made. The six inputs on the grid above show that there were three apiece for teacher and students with no student-to-student dialogue. Teacher inputs were "Warms," Initiates, and Responds while student inputs were Accepts, Amplifies, and Elicits. There was no "Cooling," Correcting, or Directing.

The reader can add many questions that could be answered by examination of a grid, and books on interaction analysis will suggest even more. For our present purposes, it is enough at this point to note that such recording of what is happening in the classroom is far more specific and helpful than a generalized teacher or student opinion that things went "pretty well" or "not so good." These grids are particularly good for testing the achievement of a teacher's objective in altering classroom patterns of interaction. A teacher who finds that he talks

80 percent of the time may wish to cut his contribution to 40 percent. Use of a grid chart will tell him accurately whether or not he is attaining this wish. It will also tell him what *kinds* of inputs he and the students are making. Except for an occasional lecture, an 80 percent teacher input seems bad in itself. But it becomes even worse when it is seen that the 20 percent student input consists mostly of responding with little or no student amplifying or initiating taking place.

Study and use of interaction analysis rationale and techniques help the teacher to (1) become aware of a wider range of possible inputs than mere presentation of facts, (2) assess his own classroom verbalizations, (3) plan ways to modify both the pattern and content of teacher-student talk, and (4) evaluate the partial or complete success or failure of his efforts. For observation and recording of data, he can make and play back for himself an audiotape or videotape recording of a class session or he can enlist the help of a supervisor or fellow teacher who could act as observer. As the classroom aggregate becomes more of a group, the threat of student evaluation becomes less, and a single student or student observer team could be used to collect data. It should not, of course, be expected that students would collect exact data. Their efforts, however, should give a rough idea of the interaction process, and their study of the categories should influence classroom give and take.

Figure 20 details an approach to the collection of interaction data which pinpoints the behavior of each member of a group. Examination of these categories will reveal that opposite behaviors are described by items 1-12, 2-11, 3-10, 4-9, 5-8, and 6-7. This would suggest that practically all the marks for any single group member would fall either between 1 and 6 *or* between 7 and 12. There may, however, be some crossing of the line as when the dominator (12) clarifies and summarizes (6) and perhaps supports the ideas of others from time to time (3). There may also be some change through time as when a nonparticipator (8) begins to participate (5).

As with all group observations that describe individual behavior, a rating sheet of this sort must be handled with care when the data is reported. If one is a dominator or a nonparticipator, one should be made aware of this and its effect on the working group. However, the information must be given in a

| NAMES | PETE | JOHN | MARY | FRED | MIKE | JEAN |
|---|---|---|---|---|---|---|
| 1. Offers direction. Helps others to share leadership. | | | | | | |
| 2. Gets the point of discussion readily. Helps others to understand. | | | | | | |
| 3. Recognizes others, supports their ideas. Disagrees without deflating status. | | | | | | |
| 4. Gives personal feelings and opinions readily. Deals readily with feelings of others. | | | | | | |
| 5. Participates in an interested manner without dominating. | | | | | | |
| 6. Clarifies and elaborates own ideas and ideas of others. Summarizes. Orients. | | | | | | |
| 7. Becomes irrelevant. Gets off track. Expresses irritation and confusion. | | | | | | |
| 8. Nonparticipator. Quiet. Withdraws from discussion. | | | | | | |
| 9. Keeps feelings hidden. Highly task oriented. "Lets get the job done!" | | | | | | |
| 10. Supports only own ideas. Disagrees with others aggressively. | | | | | | |
| 11. Constantly questioning the point of the discussion. Does not accept help. | | | | | | |
| 12. Strong directive leader. Dominates group. | | | | | | |

**Figure 20. Gorman Categories for Interaction Analysis[7]**

[7] For another approach to categorizing group interaction see Robert F. Bales, *Interaction Process Analysis: A Method for the Study of Small Groups* (Reading, Massachusetts: Addison-Wesley, 1950).

MAINTENANCE FUNCTIONS

TASK FUNCTIONS

| | Initiating Activity | Supplying Information | Giving Opinion | Requesting Information | Providing Resources | Requesting Opinion | Clarifying | Elaborating | Summarizing | Consensus Testing | Orienting | Recognizing | Accepting | Harmonizing | Compromising | Norm Testing | Communication Facilitation | Blocking |
|---|---|---|---|---|---|---|---|---|---|---|---|---|---|---|---|---|---|---|
| Alice | | | | | | | | | | | | | | | | | | |
| Betty | | | | | | | | | | | | | | | | | | |
| Clara | | | | | | | | | | | | | | | | | | |
| Doris | | | | | | | | | | | | | | | | | | |
| Edith | | | | | | | | | | | | | | | | | | |
| Frances | | | | | | | | | | | | | | | | | | |
| George | | | | | | | | | | | | | | | | | | |
| Harold | | | | | | | | | | | | | | | | | | |
| Irene | | | | | | | | | | | | | | | | | | |
| James | | | | | | | | | | | | | | | | | | |
| Kerry | | | | | | | | | | | | | | | | | | |
| Larry | | | | | | | | | | | | | | | | | | |
| Morris | | | | | | | | | | | | | | | | | | |
| Ned | | | | | | | | | | | | | | | | | | |

**Figure 21.** Task-Maintenance Checklist

helpful manner. From the beginning, the group should be made aware that the observation is part of a group self-examination—that the intent is not to label the good guys and the bad guys but rather to develop better group relationships. People who are seen as dominators are usually efficient, knowledgeable leaders. How can the group help them to emphasize this valuable contribution and play down the bossiness that often causes resentment? If John is a quiet nonparticipator, is this all due to John or is there something about the behavior of the others that is making it more difficult for John to participate? In another group he may be very talkative. Questions such as these can provide fascinating learning opportunities for all members. But there needs to be a degree of group maturity and a willingness to look objectively at one's behavior before such an instrument can be productively used.

The checklist for task and maintenance behaviors (Figure 21) can also be used by one or more observers while a group is in session. The idea, here, is to make a mark in the appropriate box describing the effects of each member's contribution. Making such a structured observation in an effective manner requires practice. If students are to make observations, they should work in pairs or trios in order to cross check each other's observations before reporting the results to the group.

The only critical item here is the last (blocking). This playing of an individual role irrelevant to the group task or maintenance needs may be deleted if the teacher feels that such a designation might have a negative effect on students so described. In many class situations there are a few students whose behavior tends to block the general progress. The other students are acutely aware of this behavior, but they do not know how to handle it, and teachers rarely teach them constructive ways of helping the blocker so that he can learn more helpful and satisfying personal behavior. As a matter of fact, some teachers themselves do not seem to know how to be helpful. As a consequence, blocking behaviors are ignored, treated with sarcasm, or met with aggressive, hostile counterbehavior (sometimes even by the teacher). A better approach is an attempt to get at the cause. If John is blocking because he feels no one is listening to him, perhaps he would respond better to being listened to than to a bawling out. He might also benefit from participation in the Listening-Helping exercise, pages 101-103.

## Personal Reaction to Class Sessions

In order to involve students in sharing responsibility for classroom success and to get data that either supports present practice or calls for change, the teacher will wish to use occasional reactionnaires. These instruments can be either open- or close-ended or a combination of both. Their items should be keyed to questions that are significant for the particular class at the particular time. Experience will help the teacher to refine the instrument so that it yields data that is of maximum help to him and to the class.

The Class Meeting Reaction sheet (Figure 22) is a simple assessment of overall class reaction to date, specific reaction to today's session, and a request for improvement ideas. The reader will note that this instrument forces the student to look at *his* part in the matter of improvement as well as that of the teacher. No signature is required so that students can feel a bit more freedom to answer frankly. The inclusion of a space for a symbol makes it possible for the teacher to compare later reactions of the same students to determine amount of change.

The two questions call for a 1-7 rating as well as a written comment for each. It should be remembered that students generally do not walk into a class with highly developed critical skills. The teacher will have to teach them how to communicate their personal reactions clearly and helpfully. Perhaps an experience in writing reactions to a film or an assembly program would prepare them for the reaction sheet. Certainly, the teacher should, in discussing the reactions, indicate better ways to respond. Thus, the second reaction sheet should be an improvement over the first as students learn better how to deal with such an assignment.

Much more close-ended and detailed is the Post Unit Reaction sheet (Figure 23). The first seven items call only for a 1-7 response, and the small space provided for high and low spots is designed to compress these answers to avoid verbosity.

In evaluating an activity such as role playing or a longer range procedure such as a student committee, the Exercise Reaction sheet (Figure 24) can be helpful in specifying the kind of response the investigator feels is necessary. This is a simple, close-ended set of items in terms of student feelings about learning, himself, and the objectives of the activity.

*Class Meeting Reaction*

In order to make the class more valuable to you, it would be helpful to know your feelings about what is going on. You need not sign the sheet, but make up a symbol which you can remember and place it on the line provided. You will use this symbol again.

Symbol _____

Circle one number for each question. #1 is extremely low; #7 is extremely high. Explain your rating on the left.

My personal reaction to the class is:     1  2  3  4  5  6  7
Comment:

My reaction to this session _____ is:     1  2  3  4  5  6  7
                            (Date)
Comment:

*For the class to improve:*

I should:                    The teacher should:

Figure 22

*Post Unit Reaction*

Symbol _____

Your frank and thoughtful reactions to the unit of teaching we have just completed should be helpful in evaluating what we have done and in planning for the future.

Circle the appropriate numbers. #1 is extremely low; #7 is extremely high.

My general reaction to this unit is:     1 2 3 4 5 6 7

My interest in the subject is:     1 2 3 4 5 6 7

My feeling about this class as a nice
place to come to is:     1 2 3 4 5 6 7

The amount of my personal learning in this unit was:     1 2 3 4 5 6 7

|  | Too Much | Too Little | Just Right |
|---|---|---|---|
| Teacher direction was | 1 2 3 | 4 5 | 6 7 |

|  | Not at all | Some | Greatly |
|---|---|---|---|
| As a result of this unit, my ability to participate has changed: | 1 2 3 | 4 5 | 6 7 |

As a result of this unit, my ability
to help in planning the course
has changed:     1 2 3 4 5 6 7

High spots of the unit were:
1.
2.
3.

Low spots of the unit were:
1.
2.
3.

Figure 23

*Exercise Reaction Sheet*

Name _____ Class _____ Group No. _____

Circle appropriate number)

|  | Little | Some | A Great Deal |
|---|---|---|---|
| In terms of subject matter I learned . . . | 1  2 | 3  4 | 5  6 |

|  | Few | Some | Many |
|---|---|---|---|
| In terms of getting to know each other, I now know . . . | 1  2 | 3  4 | 5  6 |

|  | Poorly | Well | Excel-lently |
|---|---|---|---|
| My group worked togeth-er . . . | 1  2 | 3  4 | 5  6 |

|  | Act the Same | Change Some-what | Change a Great Deal |
|---|---|---|---|
| If I could repeat the expe-rience, I would | 1  2 | 3  4 | 5  6 |

|  | Little Value | Some Value | Great Value |
|---|---|---|---|
| I now feel that getting to know others in the class is of . . . | 1  2 | 3  4 | 5  6 |

|  | Poor | Good | Excellent |
|---|---|---|---|
| My overall reaction to the experience was . . . | 1  2 | 3  4 | 5  6 |

It could be improved by:

Figure 24

*Reactionnaire*

Responding to the questions below will help to analyze and improve the activities of this class.

Symbol _____

(Circle One)

1.  What is your level of class participation?
    *Comment:*

    Low   Medium   High

2.  Is the class meeting your needs?
    *Comment:*

    Poorly   Fairly Well   Very Well

3.  How could this class be improved?

4.  What is on your mind that you wish you could say in class?

Figure 25

The Reactionnaire (Figure 25) uses the device of the symbol so that this sheet can be compared with others by the same student. It calls for his self-rating in terms of participation and asks for open-ended responses to the questions of reaction and improvement suggestions. Question four often gets at significant data by allowing students to express feelings that they may have been suppressing.

One of the best ways of handling collection of reaction data is to discuss the problem, the intent, and the way data will be handled with the class prior to passing out the sheets. There should be a willingness and a readiness on the part of the students to take part in such a research procedure. The logical outgrowth of such preparation would be for a student committee to gather, analyze, and report the data. Though they may not be ready for this the first time it is done, they should become involved shortly thereafter. If the teacher always collects and reports the data there may be some suspicion that he is manipulating the responses in order to make them come out with the "right" answers.

## Student Self-Ratings

As was noted in Figure 25, the rating of himself in terms of behavior gives a student a chance for some insightful thinking and gives the teacher some clues as to how he sees himself. Since self-concept has such a significant effect on one's continuing efforts to learn, each teacher who considers himself a professional educator must be concerned with this area of student growth. Concern all by itself, however, is not very helpful to the student. Nor is a kindly pat on the back (though such encouragement *is* important). More practical help is afforded when each student is encouraged to look insightfully at himself in terms of debits and credits, allowed to see himself at least partially through the eyes of his peers and teacher, and taught to set personal learning goals *and ways of achieving them.* One way of beginning such a program is through the use of self-reacting instruments.

The Self-Evaluation Checklist (Figure 26) gets at student perceptions of learning in different areas, knowledge of peers and teacher, types of personal behaviors supplied if any, and

*Self-Evaluation Checklist*

Symbol _____

|  | Very Little | Some-what | Very Much |
|---|---|---|---|
| 1. Were you interested in this unit? | ___ | ___ | ___ |
| 2. Did you learn content? | ___ | ___ | ___ |
| 3. Did you learn process? | ___ | ___ | ___ |
| 4. Did you learn about your strengths and weaknesses? | ___ | ___ | ___ |
| 5. Do you feel closer to your fellow students? | ___ | ___ | ___ |
| 6. Do you feel closer to the teacher? | ___ | ___ | ___ |
| 7. Did you participate? | ___ | ___ | ___ |
| 8. Did you contribute task behaviors? | ___ | ___ | ___ |
| 9. Did you contribute maintenance behaviors? | ___ | ___ | ___ |
| 10. How much leadership did you display? | ___ | ___ | ___ |

11. You have been asked to develop personal goals for learning. List three of these goals below in order of importance.
   a.
   b.
   c.

**Figure 26**

rating of personal effectiveness. In addition, it reinforces the notion of setting personal goals for learning by asking for a list of these. Such goals should be checked periodically by the student himself. As he experiments with behavior calculated to attain these goals, he will probably find that his initial statements

*A Profile of Me*

Symbol _____

How would you rate: (circle number—#1=low; #8=high)

1.  Your intelligence                      1 2 3 4 5 6 7 8
2.  Your reading ability                    1 2 3 4 5 6 7 8
3.  Your ability to express ideas
    clearly                                 1 2 3 4 5 6 7 8
4.  Your amount of class partic-
    ipation                                 1 2 3 4 5 6 7 8
5.  Your ability to get along
    with fellow students in com-
    mittee or other group work              1 2 3 4 5 6 7 8
6.  Your ability to get along
    with teachers                           1 2 3 4 5 6 7 8
7.  Your group leadership ability           1 2 3 4 5 6 7 8
8.  Your ability to keep up with
    the work of this class                  1 2 3 4 5 6 7 8
9.  Your tendency to listen to
    what the other fellow says              1 2 3 4 5 6 7 8
10. Your tendency to impress
    fellow students as a very
    worthwhile person                       1 2 3 4 5 6 7 8
11. Your tendency to recognize
    and support others in a group
    situation                               1 2 3 4 5 6 7 8
12. Your tendency to impress
    teachers as a very worthwhile
    person                                  1 2 3 4 5 6 7 8
13. Your impression of yourself
    as a very worthwhile person             1 2 3 4 5 6 7 8

Circle the numbers at the left of the three items above
which seem most important to you.

Figure 27 *(Cont. on page 193)*

What are three important things about you which are not listed above?
a.
b.
c.

Figure 27

have to be refined and rewritten. This, in itself, is an important part of the entire process.

A Profile of Me (Figure 27) moves further away from the work of this specific class and into general self-feelings. The final three items, which the student himself may fill in, often provide insight into personal concerns. Added directions for this instrument might include the circling of the three items that seem most important or most difficult for the student. Also, he may be asked to write a page or two about his feelings as a student in the school, which can be attached to the instrument.

## Ratings of Others

A group matures and becomes cohesive as members learn ways of sharing their feelings with each other in helpful ways. These feelings develop as the course moves along, and they focus on certain behaviors. If feelings—particularly negative feelings—toward the behavior of others are not shared and dealt with, they will be expressed in destructive rather than constructive ways.

Both teacher and students are concerned, and often disturbed, by the nonparticipator, who sits and says nothing; the over-participator, who is always talking even when he has nothing to say; the "boss," who tells others what to do in an authoritarian manner; and the egoist, who never seems to listen to anyone else because he is too busy paying attention to himself. Both teacher and students are concerned, but in the usual class setting, only the teacher is expected to act. Since it is also usual for the teacher to be outside the group rather than a

*Who Are These People?*

Directions: Read each description below and write the name of the student(s) it describes in the space to the right. It is possible that some names will not appear in any of these descriptions.

Symbol _____

Who is very quiet but seems to be trying?

_____

Who is a strong leader with many good ideas?

_____

Who is most willing to listen to the ideas of others?

_____

Who can explain best to those who do not understand?

_____

Who shows a serious interest in the work of the class without over-doing it?

_____

Who likes to tell others what to do?

_____

Who likes to be told what to do?

_____

Whom would you pick to see that the job gets done?

_____

Whom would you pick to make sure the group enjoyed itself?

_____

**Figure 28**

member, the whole operation of modifying behaviors is made unnecessarily difficult. What is needed is a way of helping students to share with each other their feelings about each other. The following instruments may constitute a beginning in this direction.

Responses to Who Are These People? (Figure 28) can be used to share positive student perceptions. Items focus on listening, helping, providing interest and ideas, getting the job done, and making it enjoyable. Not only will the students named in these categories feel good about it, but these qualities will be reinforced as students read them and think about them.

Negative qualities are dealt with in gentle terms in order to avoid putting people on the defensive. Such items as very quiet and strong leader, tell others what to do, and even the business of getting the job done can bring out mixed negative and positive reactions in others. Discussions based on the instrument can develop personal insights and group accord.

The reactionnaire can be given to class committees who wish to improve their work. Data can be collected by the teacher and fed back to individuals. Where the group has more cohesion and trust, a better procedure would be three minutes to react to the sheet followed by twenty minutes of sharing the data orally in small groups followed by twenty-five minutes of general class discussion concerning group building behaviors.

Where this has been done by the author, typical comments in the small groups include:

> "Well, Marty, you're a strong leader with good ideas all right, and I'm glad you're in my group. But do you ever listen to *my* ideas?"
>
> "I always look to Sam to explain things. Even the teacher sometimes confuses me, but Sam can always straighten me out."
>
> "Janice, I know you've got a lot of good things to tell the group, but you just sit there. And I think, 'How can I help her? What can I do to get her to talk? Am I doing anything to prevent her?' "

It should not tax one's imagination to guess at the impact such discussions have on students and on the class as a whole. People begin to be interested in classmates and in the subject matter to be learned. Students slowly begin to listen to each other and to see the class as more real and less of a perfunctory game ending in the Friday test, which is crammed for and promptly forgotten.

Both process *and* content form the subject of the Post-Meeting Reaction sheet (Figure 29). This sheet is given following the teaching of the concepts of content and process and immediately following a general class session or a committee meeting. Three main purposes are served. First, each student is forced to summarize what has just gone on, which should help his learning and retention. Second, he must look analytically at the process of the meeting as well as its content. Third, he must

*Post-Meeting Reaction*

Symbol _____ Date _____ Group No. _____

We have talked in class about *content* and *process* levels of communication. *Both* are *important*.

| *Content:* | The topic of conversation<br>The subject matter<br>What is talked about | *Process:* | Who says what to whom? Do people listen to each other? What is the leadership pattern? How do you feel in the group? How do members feel about the group? |
|---|---|---|---|

| Briefly describe content of session. | Briefly describe process. |
|---|---|
| | |

| What was your personal reaction to session? | What was your role? |
|---|---|
| | |

Figure 29

look at his own behavior in addition to his reaction. This third item is part of the teacher's movement toward having students share the responsibility for good learning experiences.

Group Report Reaction (Figure 30) provides helpful feedback for the group doing a report so that they may improve their operation. This is a vital activity since much classroom committee work is abandoned merely because it does not work perfectly the first time it is tried. Both teacher and students should realize that effective committee work needs to be learned through increasingly improved practice. That time spent in such learning is more than justified seems quite obvious when one considers how much work is done in committees throughout the culture and how ineffective most of this work turns out. At this point, the reader might reflect on *his* last committee participation.

In addition to providing feedback for the committees, this instrument allows each student to summarize his learnings and to develop skill in analysis or organization and presentation skills. A student who has carefully criticized a committee should tend to avoid the same mistakes when he himself becomes a member of a committee.

By reacting to the Group Evaluation (Figure 31) the student is analyzing his own group of which he is a member. How well is the group progressing? What, in my opinion, are its problems? How effective am I? How can I do more to help the group? These questions develop analysis of the group without allowing the student to stand back and ignore his own membership. Too often, a member speaks of his group in terms of what those guys are doing well or doing poorly. A major step in his learning comes when he is able to look at the group and include himself and his behavior in the general reaction.

Another potentially valuable area developed in the instrument is that of the teacher's behavior. How much is the group helped by his actions and how could he behave to be even more helpful?

Following up on the notion that evaluation during the learning is as necessary as evaluation following the learning, the Group Progress Check (Figure 32) does two things. First, it calls for a summary not only of what has been discussed and what resources are needed but also a record of action to be taken. Second, it clarifies the perceptions of the members as to what is going on. When six members of a committee all write a

*Group Report Reaction*

Members:                          Symbol _____

1. _____    2. _____    3. _____
4. _____    5. _____    6. _____

Topic:
Rate the following by circling the appropriate number.
#1 is very poor; #7 is excellent.

Content: (Was this of help to you?
         Did it extend your knowl-
         edge of the area?)          1 2 3 4 5 6 7
Comment:




Presentation: (Did the group hold
             your interest? Was the
             report clear and logi-
             cal?)                   1 2 3 4 5 6 7
Comment:




Improvement: (How could the pre-
            sentation have been improved?
            Rate low if it needs a great deal
            of improvement and high if it
            needs little.)           1 2 3 4 5 6 7

Figure 30

*Group Evaluation*

Symbol _____ Date _____ Group No. _____

| | Poor | Fair | Uncer-tain | Good | Excel-lent |
|---|---|---|---|---|---|
| My general reaction to the experience | 1 | 2 | 3 | 4 | 5 |
| Efficiency of group in doing job | 1 | 2 | 3 | 4 | 5 |
| Involvement of members in doing job | 1 | 2 | 3 | 4 | 5 |
| How effective was I? | 1 | 2 | 3 | 4 | 5 |

| Problems in group as I see them. | What I can do to help? |
|---|---|
| | |

| How effective is the teacher? | 1 | 2 | 3 | 4 | 5 |
|---|---|---|---|---|---|

How could he better meet the needs of myself and the class?

Figure 31

*Group Progress Check*

Symbol ____ Topic _____ Date _____ Group _____

Members Present

_____    _____    _____

_____    _____    _____

| Main Areas Discussed | Action |
| --- | --- |
| | |

| Resources Needed (people, materials, films) | Action |
| --- | --- |
| | |

Figure 32

different account of what has been discussed, the group learns something about the dangers of assuming that everyone has the same picture.

## Evaluation and Reaction in General

This chapter has been an attempt to further define the notion of a process level of communication in the classroom. It has included a discussion of the content level as well as process, and it has moved into the area of process evaluation. In this latter area, procedures and instruments have been suggested for the gathering of data. Finally, it has been noted that each teacher (and class) will set certain objectives that seem important to the particular situation. Thus, the material presented in this chapter will need to be adapted to individual purposes.

This is an age of students labeled as physical and psychological school dropouts, underachieving students, disadvantaged learners, and societal dropouts. It is an age of tremendous cultural and academic pressure resulting from unsettled world conditions, environmental pollution, a population explosion, and a knowledge explosion. Educators are struggling to teach more things to more people for a longer period of their lives. At a pace bewildering even to the teachers, schools are attempting to cope with the new math; the new science; the structural linguistic approach to grammar; the extension of social studies from a narrow framework of history teaching toward the inclusion of sociology, anthropology, plus the expanding spectrum of the behavioral sciences; the development of language laboratories and teaching machines; and the expansion of programs of human relations and sex education.

One result of these multi-directional explosions has been a breakdown of—or more precisely a failure to build up—effective patterns of communication in the classroom. And simultaneously with this failure has come increased student demand for identification and recognition within schooling frameworks. The Berkeley, Madison, and Columbia campus riots were caused, in great part, by student feelings of a lack of personal involvement in the university culture.

To paraphrase a familiar quotation, "Man does not live by content alone." Just as medicine advanced from a group of barbers' apprentices to the highly specialized practitioners of today, education must move in response to current demands. What has been missing in the modern teacher's preparation is a framework, or set of frameworks, for viewing, assessing, and improving communication. An important part of this lies in the affective domain. We must reach students before we can teach them, and we must help them to reach us on increasingly effective and mature levels.

# chapter 6

# Process Communication in Teaching and Learning

If the intent of the preceding chapters has been realized, there may be no need for a sixth. The reader can draw the various threads together into a garment and make the decision for himself to wear it, alter it, or discard it.

Since, however, there is a human tendency toward closure, some things should perhaps be said at this point regarding the book, its emphasis, and the educating of emotions as well as intellect. The main focus has been on affect—or process—education in the classroom.

## Where We Have Been

Throughout his centuries on the earth, man has constantly been occupied with gaining physical and emotional security. He has also accepted challenge and change as a proof that he is alive though he has striven to keep both these elements within manageable limits. Since his physical environment made more immediate, and in some ways less threatening, demands than his social environment, he began early to explore and conquer aspects of nature outside himself. His ways of dealing with his physical world became increasingly successful, and when he came to examine nature inside himself it was not surprising that he brought to bear the methods which had worked so well in nonemotional areas. Even today, "social" sciences have not completely emerged from the shadow of "physical" sciences.

In the separate subject and track curriculum approach of the schools one can see the physical science approach to the question of what a person should know and how he should come to learn it. Teacher-specialist education has followed suit, preparing "scholars" in separate disciplines. When anxiety over the quality of schooling mounts, as it has in the past generation, the overwhelming response is an increase in content and content "mastery" for both teachers and students.

This type response is in line with a cultural overemphasis on content-level communication and underemphasis on the process level. It is a little like preparing a top notch football team without locating a field for them to play on. The teacher-scholar's job is really not to show students how much *he* knows—his job is to create a dialogue so that *they* are motivated to learn and to structure experiences which will help them to learn. With John Dewey and progressive education we had one of the first humanistic challenges to rote, teacher-dominated education. Modern communication theory takes this challenge further by suggesting that we use emotions in the teaching-learning setting rather than pretend they do not exist.

The *content masters* (traditional educators) responded to available knowledge by compartmentalizing it into "subjects"; they responded to the affective side of students by creating cocurriculums; and they called for the education of specialists in guidance and school psychology. Student response is to learn bits of this and that without ever being taught to pull it all together. A common school joke concerns the student taking a social studies examination who asks if spelling counts. Spelling, after all, is an item of the English class. With guidance and psychology experts employed by schools, the inference may be made that the student should bring only his intellect to the regular classroom. His emotions will have to wait until he can get an appointment with guidance. Where the teacher goes with *his* emotions has not yet been given an institutional answer, though the question is really not a laughing matter.

Playing games of let's pretend with facts and feelings is certainly not a constructive way to live with our fellow humans. In addition, as has been pointed out on the preceding pages, it is *not* the road to good communication. The seesaw of content and process has been tipped too far for too long in the direction of content. The answer, of course, is not to tip it too far in the other direction, but to achieve a balance between the two. A first step in this direction is to create, through preservice and in-service education, a group of *content-process masters.*

This type of education would build on the teacher's prior study of content with a view toward helping him deal with cognitive *and* affective components of the learning process. It would move into four basic questions: (1) where am I now in ability to teach? (2) what is available to help me go further? (3) how can I get started? and (4) how can I evaluate my progress?

A most helpful in-service program would be the formation in a school of a twelve-member volunteer task-team which would meet weekly in two-hour sessions for ten weeks. This team would address itself to the four questions listed in the preceding paragraph, referring to texts on interaction analysis and the defining of objectives in behavioral terms as well as to texts such as this one on affect education. They would then form a mutual learning and support system for helping each other to grow as teachers, and as persons, beyond the termination date of the program. Built into the package should be a set of four follow-up sessions within a four-month period after the initial program. Far too many good beginnings are allowed to die every year because no one thinks to plan a second "shot in the arm" experience where people can take stock and plan to go ahead with ideas which develop after the finish of the first input.

Such programs for teachers, bringing in new ideas and stimulating old leadership, are a vital necessity for keeping the school alive and functioning. They get even more mileage when supervisors and administrators become a part, but not necessarily the leaders, of the learning group. Historically, much in-service education has consisted of boring lectures addressed to an already tired group whose members have put in a hard day in the classroom vineyards. If the first learning aggregate consists of volunteers, however, and if leadership can be found which will help the teacher-aggregate to begin to form a group, interest and motivation will almost certainly pick up.

Sensitivity or encounter sessions would add a great deal to group formation in an in-service program, but much can be accomplished in other ways. The theory and model of affect education put forth in this book is not sensitivity training. It proposes merely that as a learning aggregate struggles with cognitive tasks, it deals also with the feelings of members concerning themselves, the task, and the others. The careful reader of this book will realize that affect education in the classroom or in the in-service or preservice teacher program does not attempt to treat with deep, dark, psychotic expression emanating from the deep recesses of tortured souls. Groups run by specially trained guidance counselors or psychologists may attempt to provide a therapeutic experience for some students, but the general learning aggregate is subject-centered rather than therapy-centered.

The classroom aggregate-moving-toward-group needs to concentrate on the interactions of the people in the class. It is not a setting where Johnny will learn to understand his mother or discuss his sexual ambivalence, but it should not be a place where Johnny has to choke down every feeling he has about the teacher, his classmates, or the activities in which he finds himself engaged. It also should not be a place where he only rarely communicates with his peers or where his dignity is disregarded because he is only a lowly "kid" while his teacher is a lofty, unreachable adult. The teacher, on his part, will not be expected to deal in the classroom with his marriage problems or the fact that his father never hugs him. But he should be able to express his feelings of irritation regarding the discourtesy of some students in the class with the expectation that the problem will become a group problem to be faced and solved. Rather than arbitrarily changing students' seats, the group-centered teacher will express his feelings and invite students to express theirs. In this way, he will attempt to explore and solve the problem by being as mature as he can and by helping students to deal more openly and helpfully with their feelings.

## Isolation of Student Needs

Attempts to ignore the immediacy of classroom dynamics and to concentrate on meeting a variety of needs as if they could really be isolated are still being made by teachers who seem to think that people can be compartmentalized the way knowledge has been isolated in the separate subject curriculum. In this system, the classroom teacher takes care of one's intellect, guidance counselors of one's emotions, assistant principals of one's discipline, and the extracurricular program of one's social needs.

Such separation of needs makes sense when they are to be analyzed in discussion or in a textbook, but in action they need to be put back together. A carburetor, a fuel pump, and a fan belt may be taken out of the car for demonstration purposes, but it is absurd to think of them operating separately.

In similar fashion, content and process communication may be analyzed separately for discussion, yet attempting to deal with them separately at different times and different places in a school situation would be like agreeing to use the fuel pump without the carburetor today and the carburetor without the fuel pump tomorrow or to say that this Saturday we will play football without the line.

The coach knows that he has to use both the line *and* the backfield. In addition, he knows that certain linemen can receive a pass like a backfielder and that some backfielders can be used in ways similar to the line. This has a parallel in verbal interaction since various human needs not only occur simultaneously, but also overlap and intertwine. This suggests that the concept of intellectual growth is a more complicated one than teachers, or the teachers of teachers, have recognized. Members and leaders of task-centered groups know that people have social and emotional needs, but they have worked, historically, under the assumption that these needs have no direct bearing on the accomplishment of the task. Thus such needs tend to be ignored in the group, and the result is the psychological dropping out of an appreciable number of group members while the rest do most of the work. Such inefficiency, when it is recognized, is blamed on a vague scapegoat called committee work, about which countless jokes have been made (a camel is something that was put together by a committee).

## Reports and Labels

Teachers, too, are aware (at least on the intellectual level) of social needs, but they have also operated on the assumption that these have little to do with classroom learning. When failure to deal with these needs results in learning disorders, the school reacts with institutionally approved moves that neatly avoid the main issue.

Report cards and letters sent home urging parents to apply vaguely understood pressures usually increase rather than solve the problem. Children are assigned categories such as *unmotivated, underachiever, behavior problem* and are referred to non-classroom areas for help. Inherent in the material of previous chapters is the idea that most of these students might benefit most by help given in the ongoing context of the class interaction. Guidance and other areas should be used *in conjunction with* and *not apart from* the classroom. To implement this concept, the guidance counselor might be invited to visit the classroom. His expertise should be available to both teacher and students, and he should not be segregated constantly in a guidance office.

In the magnificent effort of the society to educate all its youth, many serious personality problems are bound to occur, and it would be arrant nonsense to claim that the *process* techniques suggested in the present volume constitute a panacea. But it would be even more foolish to ignore them merely because they do not solve all problems. Techniques for the development of cognitive—or *content*—communication sometimes fail, but the response to such failure has usually been to seek new ways and to improve the old. The same response ought to hold for *process* communication. When teachers realize fully that process and content are not separate and distinct, but rather form two halves of a whole called learning, many of the serious problems of schooling will begin to be solved.

## Process in Teaching

A summary of process communication in teaching should include a definition, a rationale, and some final comments on the implementation of the program.

## Content and Process

While content level has to do with the topic under discussion, process level concerns feelings that group members have about themselves and about others while the topic is being discussed. As has been seen in earlier chapters, the process level is often more hidden and more subtle than the content level. People generally have great difficulty in communicating feelings in a group setting, and the typical norm of the task-centered group is that expressions of feelings are not relevant *and should be withheld.*

Yet problems do arise between people on the feeling level. These are blockages in the process level of communication. They have nothing directly to do with the learning or the teaching of subject matter, yet they do exist and they influence the quality of learning and teaching. An irate teacher or a humiliated student cannot merely shed personal feelings like old sweaters and "get down to business." They need to explore their feelings toward themselves and each other.

Though personality clashes and behavior problems provide classroom process problems, they make up only a small percentage of process communication. The bulk of it is less upsetting and spectacular. One common problem, for example, is the lack of free response on the part of students. When the teacher asks Johnny a question he is liable, on the basis of past experience, to feel that he is being put on the spot. Instead of taking the teacher's question as an invitation to explore a content problem, the student often feels that he must recite in order to prove that he has done his homework. Thus, the quality of teacher-student interaction often has a strained, artificial overtone. As for the quality of student-student interaction, they have so little practice in traditional teacher-dominated school settings that they frequently are at a complete loss when required to carry on a class discussion. It is extremely difficult to make a group of efficient talkers out of students who have been conditioned for years to be highly dependent listeners.

Such problems have occurred, are occurring, and will continue to occur in classrooms. Solutions should be sought through exploration of alternatives rather than by rigid either-or thinking. What responses are most promising? Which would yield the least frustration and the most conflict resolution? What positive middle positions exist between too much teacher control and too much student freedom? How can students learn effective ways of sharing with the teacher the responsibility for their learning?

## Rationale for the Teaching of Process Skills

Since teaching is primarily communication, and since any communication has its content *and* process levels, improvement of teaching is directly related to improvement of communication on both these levels. Because one level is interrelated with the other, the bypassing or ignoring of the process level creates a more serious impediment to learning than has been realized until recent years. Proceeding from the assumption that process must be recognized and dealt with, techniques such as those in the present volume have been and are being developed to improve student-teacher interaction within the classroom setting.

If classroom interaction is ever to raise itself from a sort of non-life game playing, the actors on its stage are going to have to recognize themselves and the others as persons rather than objects. As should be apparent to readers of the first few chapters, however, this recognition does not come about merely through good will and determination; it requires time and the development of skills. Basic socialization processes of our culture, aided and abetted by the content preoccupation of the schools, have conditioned both students and their teachers to accept an individualized, over-intellectualized, nonemotional approach within what appears to be a group setting. The change of such expectations—or the reconditioning of the participants—requires time and patience but most of all the development of communication skills on the process level.

Time and patience—and belief in the ends being sought—are necessary because it is not enough for the teacher to announce that students are free to express themselves in this course and that they are expected to play a part in planning it, carrying it on, and evaluating it. Conditioned to play passive, listening roles, the students will not know how to use freedom and partnership with the teacher in an efficient manner. In the early stages, they will be frustrated by their inability to make group decisions and to deal competently with the subject matter in terms of defining areas of inquiry, locating resources, and using these resources. But this very frustration will generate process that can be looked at. Frustration, like any other communication problem, needs to be faced rather than avoided.

In the solving of communication problems, students will be moving from an aggregate to a group that will include the teacher as a special member. Far from losing control and respect, the teacher may become *the* most valuable group resource. The class will gradually improve in its ability to make group decisions and to set group norms of behavior. When the group accepts the freedom to develop its own norms, it will also accept the responsibility for their enforcement. The teacher will move further toward playing the role of guide to intellectual growth and further away from playing the role of law-enforcement officer. The possibilities for human fulfillment in such a group setting are most exciting. Anyone who has experienced a really free atmosphere where responsibility for control and direction are shared and where individual dignity is enhanced would never vote for a return to the baby-sitting nagging going on in too many of today's classrooms.

## Changing Behavioral Norms

In the preceding paragraphs the stress has been on (1) breaking the game-playing atmosphere to create a reality situation, (2) changing student-dependency norms, (3) helping to create an atmosphere that will reward the free expression of feelings, (4) developing shared responsibility in addition to shared freedom, and (5) creating a readiness for subject-matter learning. The purposes of the exercises detailed in the book deal with bridging the gap between the changing norms of communication. As the teaching year progresses, the exercises—as crutches—become less necessary, and the group, having become indeed a group, can address itself to the improvement of content communication. The assumption here is that process communication needs to be dealt with *before effective* content communication can take place.

The reader will note that both the words *before* and *effective* are italicized in the sentence above. The statement should *not* be read to mean that a class in history should wait for two months before beginning to learn history so that process skills can be developed. Initial efforts to learn history should begin, if not on the first day, certainly during the first week. Process and content skills should be developed together. The point made in the previous paragraph is that initial efforts on *both* levels need to be improved before effectiveness is achieved. Perhaps a better way to put it would be that both process and content communication need to be dealt with as methods of communication before effective teaching and learning can result.

This is similar to saying that communication must be improved before we can have improved communication. Such a statement could be dismissed as belaboring the obvious if it were not for the fact that communication in learning has, historically, been seen as primarily content-centered. What is new here is the focus on process communication *in addition to and combined with* content focus.

A subtle understanding problem seems to be caused by efforts—such as those in the present volume—to isolate process communication for the sake of studying it and proposing techniques to improve it. In so doing, there is the danger that it begins to be thought of as something separate and distinct from teaching the subject. Once this is done, the teacher may see it as something of a chore added to an already full day. Given a choice, he may choose to ignore it as so many teachers have done before him. In actuality, however, there is no choice. Process exists, and no one really ignores it. Whenever human beings come together to do a job such as that of the classroom they generate feelings about the job, about themselves, and about the others who are present. They may not bring these feelings out in the open where they can be handled, but the feelings are there nonetheless; they cannot be completely ignored. The basic question is not whether process should be dealt with; rather, it is *how* it should be handled.


## Aspects of Classroom Process

When one contrasts an American classroom with one in present-day Western Europe it becomes apparent that Americans deal more with process in the school. On the other hand, teachers in Western Europe are dealing more with process than did their predecessors of past generations. There seems to be a worldwide movement (evident in areas such as India as well as in the West) toward bringing the teacher more into the give-and-take of the learning group. American schools, influenced by changes in the American culture and by educational philosophers such as John

Dewey, have made giant strides toward permissiveness in the classroom and recognition of the "whole child" concept. Yet even in the United States progress has been slow. There has been a fear that freedom of student expression would result in anarchy. And this is a real problem when the teacher and students lack process skills. Allowing students freedom of expression is not really *dealing* with process; it is merely the removal of rigid controls. If substitute controls are not developed rapidly there can be classroom behavior problems. It is the failure to establish democratic controls that has caused most of the criticism of progressive education in America. As was stated above, the expectation that students who have been conditioned to be dependent will suddenly rise to the demands of a democratic situation with skill and effective behavior is asking the impossible.

The bored student who, in a free situation, tells the teacher that he is bored may be using his freedom, but he is not using it skillfully. If he had developed skill, he would have taken into account *the needs of the receiver*—in this case the teacher—and the *clarity of the message* plus his own *personal responsibility* for the boring situation. (Why did he just sit around and let it get boring?) These three aspects of process skill may be looked at in detail as follows:

*Receiver Needs*

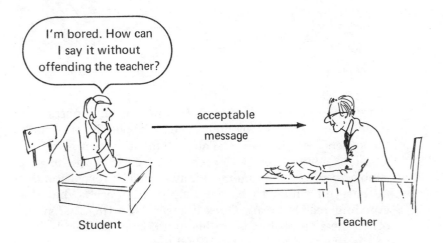

1. *Receiver needs.* Our receivers may very much need our messages. In this case the teacher needs to know that this student is bored if he is to deal with the problem. However, he also needs support and respect. Failing to receive these, he may block out or not hear the boredom message or he may feel hurt and counterattack the student, which will cause all sorts of bruised feelings *and not touch the boredom problem at all.* The student, then, has the alternative of (1) saying nothing verbally (*though the message will still come through nonverbally*), (2) saying, in a clumsy manner, that he is bored, or (3) communicating his problem to the teacher in a way that the teacher can accept without losing face and in a way that invites the teacher to help him, the student, to solve the problem.

*Clarity of Message*

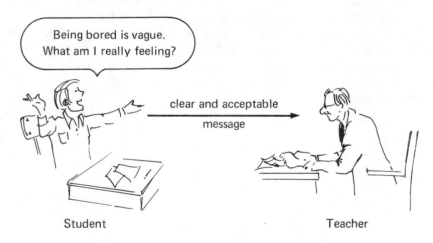

Being bored is vague. What am I really feeling?

clear and acceptable message

Student                    Teacher

2. *Clarity of message.* The need for training in process communication becomes evident whenever people attempt to tell others how they feel. The statement, "I am bored," is a case in point. Even if the teacher-receiver of this message is able to react to it unemotionally, what information does he have on which to base a helpful response? What does boredom really mean? Does it mean that the student has other pressing problems on his mind, that he feels left out of the group, that he has finished the work and has nothing

to do, that he does not know how to do the work and is frustrated, or does it mean something else? Until the teacher knows more than the bare word *boredom*, he is not in any position to help.

## Personal Responsibility

I'm glad now that I told him I was bored. I must have done it with some skill. He doesn't seem offended.

We seem to be getting somewhere. Last year I would have cut a student down for even hinting he was bored.

Maybe I should do something about my boredom. Why blame it all on him?

It helped me that he said it gently. I'm proud that I handled it positively.

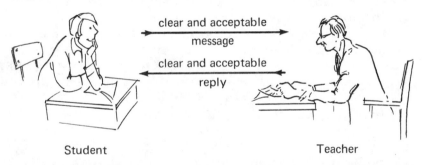

clear and acceptable message

clear and acceptable reply

Student                                     Teacher

3. *Personal responsibility.* Good teachers do not evade their responsibility for the success of the class—or, more precisely, for the success of each student within the class—but students evade this constantly. In fact, most students do not seem to recognize that there is any sphere of responsibility that *is* theirs. This can be blamed on traditional teacher domination, but it seems sad and fruitless to dash about looking for someone to blame. As process skills are developed, the learning group and its teacher will begin to recognize a joint responsibility. And this, in turn, will help the two aspects detailed above under needs and clarity. If there is a joint responsibility, a student will be able to tell a teacher—or for that matter, a classmate—that he is bored

without producing a defensive reaction on the part of the teacher. Rather than feeling offended or made a scapegoat, the teacher now will be free to react as he might to any request for help.

To test out the need for process skills, the reader should think of the most democratic classroom he has himself experienced and ask himself questions such as the following: "How free were the students to say what they really felt?" "How much personal responsibility did students feel for the success of the class?" "How much student-student interaction was there?" "To what degree was the teacher a member of the group?"

## The Process Role of the Teacher

It is important for the classroom teacher who wishes to approach process communication in more than a hit or miss fashion to understand that he is *not* engaging in clinical psychology. Deep-seated emotional problems are not the business of the classroom. It is not within the scope of schooling objectives to probe people's psyches. This fact, however, should not serve the teacher as an excuse for dodging the problem of process awareness and process analysis in the classroom.

Careful examination of the procedures discussed in the previous chapters will show that the main effort is directed at freeing the expressions of feelings that are already present and are probably being expressed unclearly and nonverbally. Such feelings (on the part of the teacher as well as student) not only affect what goes on in the class, but affect it in non-helpful ways. The emphasis of the present book is on bringing out and clarifying feelings; on building supporting norms for open, spontaneous behavior; and on developing verbal communication skills. In such classrooms, your best friend *will* tell you, and he will tell you in a clear, supportive, helpful way.

Teachers need not be psychologists, but they do need more education in the guidance area both in terms of skill and of the guidance point of view. The techniques detailed in the preceding chapters should provide a solid groundwork for further exploration of process communication *and* of its close inter-relationship to content communication.

What is needed to bring teacher effectiveness closer to the point where it can be considered truly professional is a revision of the traditionally muddled thinking concerning the teaching-learning operation. Process communication is not seen by a real professional as just one more nice little fad to be used when and if there is nothing else going on. Rather, it is seen as an integral part of content communication so that one cannot really be said to exist independent of the other. The whole child does indeed come into the classroom, *and the whole teacher comes in as well.*

## Interaction Theory and Schooling

This interrelationship of communication levels set within a clearly thought-through theory of interaction is what the so-called guidance point of view has been struggling with throughout this century. What has been lacking is an integrated operational concept for the school, which would clearly delineate the duties, responsibilities, and spheres of influence of classroom teachers, guidance counselors, deans, and school psychologists.

The spelling out of these interlocking operations will be the task of a future book. Present purposes are served by the focus on the classroom social system. The best type of summary for this book would be a careful rereading followed by classroom tryouts of some of the procedures suggested. After doing this, the reader may compare his findings with the following in order to get a feeling of fitting the various pieces into an organic picture of schooling:

1. The American school and its society is undergoing physical and psychological change.
2. The physical change relates to population and knowledge explosions, which require accompanying changes in physical plant, staff, and curriculum organization.
3. The psychological change relates to increasing awareness of and demand for more openness in human communication.
4. Teaching and learning has been, historically, a teacher-dominated, one-way process composed of active teachers

and passive learners. This posture on the part of the school will change more slowly than the expressed needs in the general culture, but it *will* change.

5. Agents of this change will be teachers and administrators working out of frameworks such as the one described in this book.

6. Teaching will be more tightly related to teaching theory as more knowledge becomes available concerning the behavioral outcomes of different teaching approaches.

7. Much of this knowledge will come from action research carried out at the classroom level by teachers who experiment with both process and content levels of communication in teaching.

Throughout this book the author has made a conscious effort to communicate with the reader on a direct and personal level. He has tried to anticipate process reactions of the reader and to discuss these thoroughly. On the content level, he has begun by attempting a rationale and conceptual framework underlying the interactive process of teaching and learning; has moved on to spell out, step-by-step, classroom-tested procedures that may be used to cut through the communication barriers that have historically interfered with in-depth learning; has discussed and illustrated the problems of and procedures for gathering data concerning the success or failure of process activities; and has, finally, pulled at least some of the school and societal threads together to show the forces at work to move schooling from its traditional preoccupation with content communication toward a focus on *both content and process*.

What happens at this point is in the hands of the book's readers. Process analysis, with its opening up of human feelings, can be quite threatening, but it can also create a marvelous feeling of rapport and progress that lifts teaching to truly professional levels. It is time to stop cheating students (and teachers) out of a complete educational experience. If the contents of the present volume prove helpful to teachers who are looking for ways to increase the meaningfulness of student experience it will have fulfilled its purpose.

# Bibliography

Entries marked with an asterisk (*) deal specifically with interaction analysis. Those marked with a dagger (†) deal with affect education and sensitivity training.

*Amidon, Edmund J. *The Role of the Teacher in the Classroom.* Minneapolis: Association for Productive Teaching, 1967.

*——, and John B. Hough. *Interaction Analysis: Theory, Research and Application.* Reading, Mass.: Addison-Wesley Publishing Co., 1967.

*——, and Elizabeth Hunter. *Improving Teaching: Analyzing Verbal Interaction in the Classroom.* New York: Holt, Rinehart and Winston, Inc., 1966.

*——, and Anita Simon. "Teacher-Pupil Interaction." *Review of Educational Research,* vol. 35, no. 2.

*——, and Ned Flanders. *The Role of the Teacher in the Classroom: A Manual for Understanding and Improving Teachers' Classroom Behavior.* Minneapolis: Paul S. Amidon and Associates, 1963.

Andrews, Kenneth R., ed. *The Case Method of Teaching Human Relations and Administration.* Cambridge, Mass.: Harvard University Press, 1960.

Argyris, Chris. *Organization and Innovation.* New York: Dorsey Press, 1965.

Association for Supervision and Curriculum Development. *Theories of Instruction.* Washington, D.C.: The Association, 1965.

——. *Perceiving, Behaving, Becoming.* Yearbook. Washington, D.C.: The Association, 1962.

———. *Toward Better Teaching: A Report of Current Practices.* Yearbook. Washington, D.C.: The Association, 1949.

*Bales, Robert F. *Interaction Process Analysis.* Reading, Mass.: Addison-Wesley Publishing Co., 1950.

Beal, George M., Joe M. Bohlen, and J. Neil Raudabaugh. *Leadership and Dynamic Group Action.* Ames, Iowa: Iowa State University Press, 1962.

Beckhard, Richard. *Organization Development: Strategies and Models.* Reading, Mass.: Addison-Wesley Publishing Co., 1966.

*Bellack, Arno A. *Theory and Research in Teaching.* New York: Bureau of Publications, Teachers College, Columbia University, 1963.

†Benne, Kenneth D., and Paul Sheats. "Functional Roles of Group Members." *Journal of Social Issues*, vol. 4, no. 2:41-49.

Bernard, Harold W. *Mental Health in the Classroom.* New York: McGraw-Hill Book Co., 1970.

†Berne, Eric. *Games People Play: The Psychology of Human Relationships.* New York: Grove Press, Inc., 1964.

———. *The Structure and Dynamics of Organizations and Groups.* New York: Grove Press, Inc., 1963.

Biddle, Bruce J., and William J. Ellena, eds. *Contemporary Research on Teacher Effectiveness.* New York: Holt, Rinehart and Winston, 1964.

†Bion, Wilfred R. *Experiences in Groups and Other Papers.* London: Tavistock Publications, 1961.

†Borton, Terry. *Reach, Touch, Teach.* New York: McGraw-Hill Book Co., 1970.

†Bowers, Norman D., and Robert S. Soar. *Studies of Human Relations in the Teaching-Learning Process.* V. Final Report: Evaluation of Laboratory Human Relations Training for Classroom Teachers. U.S. Department of Health, Education and Welfare, Office of Education. Cooperative Research Project n. 496. Chapel Hill, North Carolina: University of North Carolina, 1961.

*———, and Robert S. Soar. "The Influence of Teacher Personality on Classroom Interaction." *Journal of Experimental Education*, vol. 30 (June 1962).

†Bradford, Leland P., Jack R. Gibb, and Kenneth D. Benne, eds. *T-Group Theory and Laboratory Method.* New York: John Wiley and Sons, Inc., 1964.

Branden, Nathaniel. *The Psychology of Self-Esteem.* Los Angeles: Nash Publishing Corp., 1969.

†Brown, George I. *Human Teaching for Human Learning: An Introduction to Confluent Education.* New York: The Viking Press, 1971.

†Burton, Arthur, ed. *Encounter*. San Francisco: Jossey-Bass Inc., Publishers, 1970.

Cantor, Nathaniel. *The Dynamics of Learning*, 2d ed. Buffalo, N.Y.: Foster and Steward, 1950.

Clark, Donald M., and Asya L. Kadis. *Humanistic Teaching*. Columbus, Ohio: Charles E. Merrill Publishing Co., 1971.

Coleman, James S. *The Adolescent Society: The Social Life of the Teenager and Its Impact on Education*. New York: Free Press, 1961.

Collins, Barry E., and Harold Guetzkow. *A Social Psychology of Group Processes for Decision Making*. New York: John Wiley and Sons, Inc., 1964.

†Egan, Gerard. *Encounter: Group Processes for Interpersonal Growth*. Belmont, Calif.: Brooks/Cole Publishing Co., 1970.

†Fast, Julius. *Body Language*. New York: M. Evans and Co., Inc., 1970.

*Fattu, N. A. "Explorations of Interactions Among Instruction, Content and Aptitude Variables." *Journal of Teacher Education*, vol. 14, no. 3 (September 1963).

*Flanders, Ned A. *Interaction Analysis in the Classroom: A Manual for Observers*. Ann Arbor, Mich.: The University of Michigan, 1966.

Fox, Robert S., *Inventory of Teaching Innovations Directed Toward Improving Classroom Learning Atmospheres*. Ann Arbor, Mich.: Institute for Social Research, University of Michigan, 1961.

———, and Ronald Lippitt. "The Innovation of Classroom Mental Health Practices." In Matthew B. Miles, *Innovation in Education*. New York: Bureau of Publications, Teachers College, Columbia University, 1964.

Gabriel, John. *An Analysis of the Emotional Problems of the Teacher in the Classroom*. Melbourne: F. W. Chesire, 1957.

*Gage, Nathaniel L., Philip J. Runkel, and B. B. Chatterjee. *Equilibrium Theory and Behavior Change: An Experiment in Feedback from Pupils to Teachers*. Urbana, Ill.: Bureau of Educational Research, College of Education, University of Illinois, 1960.

Garrett, Henry E. *The Art of Good Teaching*. New York: D. McKay Co., 1964.

†Gibb, Jack R., Grace N. Platts, and Lorraine F. Miller. *Dynamics of Participative Groups*. Boulder, Colorado: University of Colorado, 1951.

†———, and Lorraine M. Gibb, eds. "Spotlight on Members' Roles." *Adult Leadership*, vol. 1, no. 8:2-23.

†Golembiewski, Robert T., and Arthur Blumberg. *Sensitivity Training and the Laboratory Approach*. Itasca, Ill.: F. E. Peacock, Publishers, Inc., 1970.

†————. *The Small Group: An Analysis of Research Concepts and Operations.* Chicago: University of Chicago Press, 1962.

†Gorman, Alfred H. *The Leader in the Group.* New York: Bureau of Publications, Teachers College, Columbia University, 1963.

Gronlund, Norman E. *Sociometry in the Classroom.* New York: Harper, 1959.

†Hamachek, Don E. *Encounters with the Self.* New York: Holt, Rinehart and Winston, Inc., 1971.

Hare, Paul. *Handbook of Small Group Research.* New York: The Free Press, 1966.

†Harris, Thomas A. *I'm O.K.—You're O.K.: A Practical Guide to Transactional Analysis.* New York: Harper and Row, 1969.

Harvey, O. J. *Motivation and Social Interaction: Cognitive Determinants.* New York: Ronald Press Co., 1963.

Hillson, Maurice, and Ronald T. Hyman, eds. *Change and Innovation in Elementary and Secondary Organization.* New York: Holt, Rinehart and Winston, 1971.

*Honigman, Fred K. "Multidimensional Analysis of Classroom Interaction (MAC)." Villanova, Pa.: Villanova University Press, 1967.

†Howard, Jane. *Please Touch.* New York: McGraw-Hill Book Co., 1970.

Hughes, Marie, et al. *Development of the Means for Assessment of the Quality of Teaching in Elementary Schools.* Salt Lake City: University of Utah, 1959.

Huxley, Aldous. *Brave New World.* New York: Harper, 1946.

Johnston, Bernard. *The Literature of Learning.* New York: Holt, Rinehart and Winston, Inc., 1971.

†Jourard, Sydney M. *The Transparent Self.* Princeton, N.J.: D. Van Nostrand, 1964.

Kaufman, Bel. *Up the Down Staircase.* Englewood Cliffs, N.J.: Prentice-Hall, Inc., 1964.

†Kemp, C. Gratton. *Perspectives on the Group Process,* 2d ed. Boston: Houghton Mifflin Co., 1970.

Klein, Alan F. *Role Playing in Leadership Training and Group Problem Solving.* New York: Association Press, 1956.

Klein, Josephine. *Working with Groups: The Social Psychology of Discussion and Decision.* London: Hutchinson University Library, 1963.

Kohl, Herbert. *36 Children.* New York: New American Library, 1967.

*Kounin, Jacob S., Paul V. Gump, and James J. Ryan. "Explorations in Classroom Management." *Journal of Teacher Education,* vol. 12, no. 2.

Kozol, Jonathan. *Death at an Early Age.* Boston: Houghton Mifflin Co., 1967.

Leonard, George B. *Education and Ecstasy.* New York: Dell Publishing Co., 1969.

Lewis, Sinclair. *Babbitt.* New York: Harcourt, 1950.

Lippitt, Ronald, and Elmer Van Egmond, eds. *Inventory of Classroom Study Tools for Understanding and Improving Classroom Learning Processes.* Ann Arbor, Mich.: Institute for Social Research, University of Michigan, 1962.

———, and Ralph K. White. "The Social Climate of Children's Groups." In Robert Barker, Jacob Kounin, and Herbert Wright, *Child Development and Behavior.* New York: McGraw-Hill Book Co., 1943.

Llewellyn, Ardelle, and David Cahoon. "Teaching for Affective Learning." *Educational Leadership,* vol. 22, no. 7.

Lott, Albert J., and Bernice E. Lott. *The Influence of Classroom Group Cohesiveness on Learning and Adherence to Standards.* Lexington, Kentucky: Research Foundation, University of Kentucky, 1964.

†Luft, Joseph. *Group Processes: An Introduction to Group Dynamics,* 2d ed. Palo Alto, Calif.: National Press Books, 1970.

Lysaught, Jerome P., and Clarence Williams. *A Guide to Programmed Instruction.* New York: Wiley, 1963.

Mager, Robert F. *Preparing Objectives for Programmed Instruction.* San Francisco: Fearon Pubs., 1962.

†Maslow, Abraham H. *Toward a Psychology of Being.* New York: Van Nostrand Reinhold Co., 1968.

*Medley, Donald M. "The Language of Teacher Behavior: Communicating the Results of Structured Observations to Teachers." Paper presented at the annual meeting of The American Educational Research Association, Chicago. February 18, 1967.

*———. "The Scientific Study of Teacher Behavior." In *Theory and Research in Teacher Education,* ed. Arno A. Bellack. New York: Bureau of Publications, Teachers College, Columbia University, 1963.

*———, and Harold E. Mitzel. "A Technique for Measuring Classroom Behavior." *Journal of Educational Psychology,* vol. 49 (April 1958).

McGrath, Joseph E., and Irwin Altman. *Small Group Research.* New York: Holt, Rinehart, and Winston, Inc., 1966.

McGregor, Douglas. *The Human Side of Enterprise.* New York: McGraw-Hill Book Co., 1969.

†Miles, Matthew B. *Learning to Work in Groups.* New York: Bureau of Publications, Teachers College, Columbia University, 1959.

*Mirrors for Behavior, An Anthology of Classroom Observation Instruments.* Research for Better Schools, Inc. and the Center for the Study of Teaching, eds. Anita Simon and E. Gil Boyer. Philadelphia: Temple University Press, 1967.

*Morrison, Virginia B. *Classroom Control and Discipline Schedule.* Rochester, Mich.: School of Education, Oakland University, 1970.

*———, and John Childs. "Strategies for the Application of Videotape in Teacher Education." *Audiovisual Instruction* (March 1969).

†Moustakas, Clark E. *The Authentic Teacher; Sensitivity and Awareness in the Classroom.* Cambridge, Mass.: Howard A. Doyle Publishing Co., 1966.

———. *The Self.* New York: Harper and Row, 1956.

National Society of the Study of Education. *The Dynamics of Instructional Groups: Sociopsychological Aspects of Teaching and Learning.* The 59th Yearbook, Part 2, ed. Newson B. Henry. Chicago: University of Chicago Press, 1960.

*Ober, Richard L., Ernest L. Bentley, and Edith Miller. *Systematic Observation of Teaching: An Interaction Analysis—Instructional Strategy Approach.* Englewood Cliffs, N.J.: Prentice-Hall, Inc., 1971.

Olmsted, Michael S. *The Small Group.* New York: Random House, 1959.

*Openshaw, M. Karl, and Frederick R. Cyphert. *The Development of a Taxonomy for the Classification of Teacher Classroom Behavior,* CRP #2288. Columbus, Ohio: Ohio State University Research Foundations, 1966.

Orwell, George. *1984.* New York: Harcourt, 1949.

Osborn, Alex F. *Applied Imagination: Principles and Procedures of Creative Problem-Solving.* New York: Charles Scribner's Sons, 1963.

*Perkins, Hugh. "Procedures for Assessing the Classroom Behaviors of Students and Teachers." *American Educational Research Journal* (November 1964).

†Pfeiffer, J. William, and John E. Jones. *A Handbook of Structured Experiences for Human Relations Training,* vols. 1-3. Iowa City: Iowa University Associates Press, 1970.

†Postman, Neil, and Charles Weingartner. *The Soft Revolution.* New York. Dell Publishing Co., Inc., 1971.

———. *Teaching as a Subversive Activity.* New York: Dell Publishing Co., Inc., 1969.

†Powell, John S. J. *Why am i afraid to tell you who i am?* Chicago: Peacock Books, 1969.

Raths, Louis E., Merrill Harmin, and Sidney B. Simon. *Values and Teaching.* Columbus, Ohio: Charles E. Merrill, 1966.

Reisman, David. *The Lonely Crowd.* New Haven, Conn.: Yale University Press, 1950.

Roethlisberger, Fritz J. *The Human Problems of an Industrial Civilization.* New York: Viking Press, 1960.

†Rogers, Carl. *Carl Rogers on Encounter Groups.* New York: Harper and Row, 1970.

†———. *Freedom to Learn.* Columbus, Ohio: Charles E. Merrill Co., 1969.

Schmuck, Richard, and Matthew B. Miles. *Organizational Development in Schools.* Palo Alto, Calif.: National Press Books, 1971.

†Schutz, William C. *Here Comes Everybody.* New York: Harper and Row, Publishers, 1971.

†———. *Joy: Expanding Human Awareness.* New York: Grove Press, Inc., 1967.

†Shepard, Martin, and Marjorie Lee. *Marathon 16.* New York: G. Putnam Sons, 1970.

†Siroka, Robert W., Ellen K. Siroka, and Gilbert A. Schloss. *Sensitivity Training and Group Encounter.* New York: Grosset and Dunlap, 1971.

Skinner, Burrus F. *The Technology of Teaching.* New York: Appleton-Century-Crofts, 1968.

Smith, B. Othanel, and Milton O. Meux. *A Study of the Logic of Teaching.* Urbana, Ill.: University of Illinois, 1963.

Snygg, Donald, and Arthur W. Combs. *Individual Behavior: A Perceptual Approach to Behavior.* New York: Harper, 1959.

Tanner, Laurel N., and Henry Clay Lindgren. *Classroom Teaching and Learning: A Mental Health Approach.* New York: Holt, Rinehart and Winston, Inc., 1971.

*Thelan, Herbert. "Insights for Teaching from a Theory of Interaction." *The Nature of Teaching.* Milwaukee, Wisconsin: University of Wisconsin, 1963.

Watson, Goodwin. *Social Psychology: Issues and Insights.* Philadelphia: J. B. Lippincott, 1965.

†Weinstein, Gerald, and Mario D. Fantini, eds. *Toward Humanistic Education: A Curriculum of Affect.* New York: Praeger Publishers, 1970.

Williams, Emlyn. *The Corn Is Green.* New York: Random House, 1941.

# Index